It's Time to Get Cheap, Girl

Bonnie Winters

with Jeremy Bradley

THIS ONE'S FOR YOU

We are so overwhelmed by the glitz and glamor of the celebrity lifestyle, but how often is the emphasis put on being cheap? Some people try to gussy it up by calling it "thrifty" but isn't that just a rich person's cover-up to not sound like a regular person? Embrace your inner cheapskate, girl. Be proud of every penny you save.

CONTENTS

IT'S TIME TO GET CHEAP, GIRL

WELCOME, CHEAP GIRLS!

We live in a world where it's all about the price you paid for things. And if you can't afford the high-priced items you are meant to feel like you should be making more money or have to get another job. This book is ready to empower you and encourage you to embrace your inner cheapskate.

I am by no means a money expert. I'll be the first to admit I'm just someone who values every dollar I have.

Like many people, I have worked hard for my money. When the economic crisis hit a few years ago, I wasn't personally affected by any financial struggles but I began assessing the ins and outs of my money.

Don't get me wrong, I wasn't always a penny pincher. When I was a teenager living with my parents I was spending recklessly and visiting a casino a few times a week and had no problem blowing a hundred bucks in twenty minutes.

Then it was time to grow up and be on my own with a house and other major expenses and I started getting creative with my funds – and I actually began having fun with it.

This isn't a book telling you how to get rich quick or ways to retire early. It is simply a compilation of things I have done in my life to reduce expenses. There is no miracle trick or big risk to take, these are all regular things almost anybody can do. You might not think a few pennies here and there is a huge deal, but when you reassess where the pennies are going and how you can hang on to more of them, you will be surprised how soon they stack up.

I have never gone hungry, I have never declared bankruptcy, but I live comfortably in a nice house and have everything I want.

People often think saving means that you deprive yourself of the fun things in life. I have come up with many ways to not only have fun with money, but also appreciate it. I'll give you the tidbits I consciously came up with and some I stumbled upon in my day-to-day life and thought, Hey, this is a really good idea.

Yes, there are ways to take a luxury vacation without having to get another mortgage. Yes, you can get things for free just by asking.

When you have a problem with a company are you a complainer or a negotiator? There is a huge difference and you'll see why.

These are all common-sense tactics for getting through life. Well, they might not be common sense to you now, but after flipping through these pages and doing some creative thinking, you'll see saving can be sexy.

This book isn't just about saving. There is a large part of this text that will tell you how to make money. Whether it is a hobby that keeps you busy a few hours a week or making a business out of garage sales, you can make money – meaning, profit – from such activities. It can be done.

FAMILY SAVINGS

WEEKENDS ON THE CHEAP

The most expensive time of the week for some: weekends. Weekends are a wallet buster – or at least a wallet emptier. But weekends can be incredibly cheap and extremely fun when you involve some creativity.

There's nothing wrong with saving up and having a lavish weekend of pampering and extravagance. Maybe it is during a holiday weekend or a birthday or an anniversary. Remember, not every weekend has to have the glitz and glamor of a Hollywood lifestyle.

Whether you are a single, a couple or a couple with kids, there are things you can do to save money and still have a good time. And as dopey as some of the ideas might seem now, give them a shot and then see if you have changed your opinion.

One of my favorites is to make pizza. Sure, it might sound simple, but when you think about how much it costs to order a pie loaded with toppings and have it delivered (especially when you're feeding more than one person) it can easily cost twenty dollars or even fifty dollars, thanks to delivery and debit card fees.

Stores have do-it-yourself kits. For five dollars I get two pizza crusts and packages of sauce and I can run wild buying fresh toppings and cheese to have pizza night. All told, two pizzas cost about eight dollars to make.

Now that Friday dinner is taken care of, what's the entertainment for the night? You can't go wrong with digging out the old VHS tapes and watching classic shows you taped years ago. Have a home video to watch? Remember Aunt Berta's fiftieth birthday party decades ago? Put that on and laugh at the hairstyles and clothes from back in the day. Talk about priceless! And while you're at it, convert those VCR tapes into digital files. There are free programs online that can help you with that.

So you fell asleep in the living room watching videos and wake up Saturday morning. Breakfast might be that leftover pizza. OK, it's not the healthiest choice, but it's the weekend, so why not?

Ease into the day taking care of the little household chores you have been putting off. That kitchen cupboard door hanging by one hinge – dig out the screwdriver, it's a quick fix, anyway. The laundry you didn't fold a few days ago is waiting for attention. Remember that picture you bought but never did hang up? There's no better time!

Once you get into a fix-it/cleaning mode, you might be on a roll to keep going. It's amazing how Saturday afternoon can be – dare I say it – productive!

And for supper, you can't go wrong raiding the produce section of fresh veggies and some low-fat dip and cheeses and having a mini buffet of healthy goodness. Think of all those people hitting up the ATMs for a stack of twenties for bad food and watery booze at the bar.

What's the plan for Saturday night? While others are hitting up a club and going dancing, why not dust off the tapes or CDs and have a homemade dance party? Seriously, it can be great fun (and cheap, remember) to entertain yourself and dim the lights or turn them off altogether and have some flashlights around the room and make your own club. Quit laughing at the idea because before you know it you'll remember all the classic songs you used to love and work up a sweat dancing for hours.

Oh, Sunday; A day to sleep away the morning and do nothing. Map out a food plan for the week and pick some outfits for work or school and prepare for the days ahead. Check in with the world on Facebook and make up a glamorous story about how you spent your weekend and get a conversation going online. Sure, spend a few hours sitting in front of the computer. After all, you stayed away from it the whole weekend, right?

If the weather is nice go for a walk. You might be surprised the different parts of the community you discover when you go exploring. Oftentimes there's a hidden park tucked away amongst the streets and houses. Kids will be getting exercise, the dog will be chasing the ball you are throwing across the field – a very active time for the whole family.

Monday rolls around and the water cooler talk is about how messed up people got on the weekend and you have a smile because you saved money, had a good time and didn't face any embarrassment with drunken pictures posted online. Cheap weekends really can be fun.

ENJOYING A LONG WEEKEND

It is the first long weekend of the summer. And with gas prices traditionally soaring this time of year, it could either make for a really expensive weekend or a weekend spent close to home.

Remember, money doesn't always make a weekend. There are plenty of things to do on a long weekend that don't have to cost you money. In fact, you might even be able to make some money.

You're stuck at home because you don't want to fill up the tank. And with summer weather happening, there's no better time to have a garage sale. Or, get crafty. We'll have chapters about that later in the book. Gather some old magazines and find some colorful pictures in them and make a collage of the photographs.

One idea – thanks to a school project from back in the day – is accordion-folding a page and tying it in the middle to make a butterfly. When you are done, set up a table outside and sell your art.

There's nothing like a day at the beach on a hot day. Bring the beach to your yard. Find some large garbage bags, cut them up and get out the garden hose. You'd be surprised how much fun slipping and sliding in the backyard can be. Add some dish soap for extra slip. Another tip is to get some foaming bath gel and get the bubbles flying and have a foam party. (One safety tip: remove twigs and branches to avoid cuts and scratches.)

Without the expense of filling up the propane barbecue, use a fire pit and roast some potatoes and other vegetables. Earlier you collected twigs and branches from the yard – they are needed to start your fire!

With it becoming increasingly easier to sit around and do nothing, the nice weather is a perfect excuse to get out and be active. Walk the dog, take the kids to the park. Better yet, get a pedometer and track your travels. It doesn't have to be a long walk, just doing chores around the house will add up your steps. You might be able to clock five miles in a day and not even realize it. The next day, try log six miles.

After getting a little too much sun you retreat inside for some shade. You remember there's that closet of old photo albums, and a walk down memory lane is just what you need while sipping on a cool drink. After the picture recap, it's not a bad idea to go through the digital camera memory cards and create a slideshow, or mark pictures for printing to create an updated album.

Not that you have to be the crafty type, but one idea for a creative photo album is placing two similar pictures side by side – that old snapshot of Aunt Greta at a wedding in the nineteen-seventies and the updated snapshot of Aunt Greta at a wedding last year. It's interesting to see how people change. (What was with that hair?!?!) Sure, it might be a laugh at Aunt Greta's expense, but it is a good time nonetheless.

Have you ever surfed YouTube for a specific video but been sidetracked by "related matches" or other previews shown on the results page? It happens to me all the time and it can lead to hours of distraction. Whether it is watching clips of classic TV shows or newscast bloopers or funny pet moments, you can end up viewing a couple dozen videos before realizing you still haven't watched the initial clip you initially searched for.

Either way, distracted or not, you still kept yourself entertained and it killed a bit of time and didn't cost you anything. Cheaper than renting a movie on pay-per-view, the Internet can be a wonderful place and a great source of entertainment.

These are just a few ideas to keep your weekend enjoyable. Have a cheap long weekend – hey, that's not a bad thing!

COUNT YOUR COUPONS

Your salary isn't going up but the cost of gas and groceries is. What do you do? The kids have to eat and you have to get to work.

Aside from starving yourself to ensure you can feed your children, there are things to consider when hitting the supermarket. What I first did when I moved out on my own was load up on groceries and fill the fridge and cupboards. I was an ambitious grocery shopper only to have much of the food go to waste since I didn't eat it fast enough.

Now I make sure I eat everything in the kitchen before shopping for more. It is easy to have a freezer full of food and go shopping for more when you still haven't eaten what you bought weeks ago. Damn those cravings! I make sure there is no food in the freezer when I visit the store. This forces me to eat what I already bought but also punish me for buying the things I didn't want to eat in the first place. And I am too stubborn to throw out perfectly good food so I am bound to eat it, anyway.

With the cupboards bare and the fridge echoing when you open the door, it is the perfect time to stock up.

Coupons, coupons, coupons. Fifty cents here, buy one get one free there – it adds up over the course of a year.

Think about it: if you grocery shop once per week and use five coupons that save you five dollars every time, that's a savings of two-hundred-sixty dollars over the course of a year. It might not seem like much, but once you get into the habit of saving you'll be excited about finding the latest deals so you can hang onto your money.

When it comes to coupons, it's worth asking if a store will accept a competitor's coupons. Lots of stores match a competitor's price, but what about accepting the competitor's coupons? Ask around and you'd be surprised how many stores will do it.

Grocery stores often run the same specials on a rotation. If crackers were on sale last week chances are if you wait a few more weeks you'll catch another great sale, if not the exact same one.

Some stores follow the "Scanning Code of Practice" which means if an item is mislabeled and scans at a higher price than the shelf label, you get the item free (up to ten dollars). Nearly every time I shop I end up getting something free.

For weeks I got a small bag of dog food free because it was labeled at nine dollars but scanned at twelve dollars and staff never changed the label. I continuously bought that brand because I knew I would get it free.

I will admit I was one of those people who mocked the customers that stared at the register's display and watched every item get scanned but it really does save you money. Many is a time I laughed at my mom for arguing with the cashier and holding up a line while an employee did a price check. Now my mom is taking notes from me. She had no idea about the Scanning Code of Practice and now is excited when I get stuff for free. (A side note: she has tried to get the same item free the next day but staff already took down the incorrect label!)

A lot of times we are enticed to buy in multiples (you've seen the signs: "two for five dollars") but if you don't need two, find out if the individual price is still discounted – oftentimes it is. Most of the time the store is banking on you getting suckered into buying more, but now you know better.

Buying items on sale and storing them – freezable items, canned goods – will benefit you in the long run. When cans of soup are on sale, I stock up even though I don't eat soup very often. But when I get sick, I know I will have food to get me through the tough time.

Fresh chicken can be expensive but buying a big box of frozen chicken breasts can be much cheaper. Taking it one step further, if the store sells a bag of frozen chicken breasts, look for a larger box of it. I recently saw a two-kilogram bag of chicken breasts for twenty-two dollars. Just down the aisle on a bottom shelf was a white box with no flashy label or packaging. It was a four-kilogram box of the same thing for twenty-six dollars. I got double the amount of chicken for an extra four dollars. Thankfully I love chicken so it's not that I was buying a larger quantity simply because it was cheap.

Watch for markdowns! Just the other day at the store I noticed big blocks of cheese were marked down. I checked the best before date and it was two months away. I asked the cashier why it was marked down and she said it was an overstock shipment and they tossed it in the dairy case to be cleared out. I saved four dollars on it because the store had too much.

Make it yourself. As I already mentioned, ordering a pizza or even buying a ready-made pizza can set you back a fair bit. Buying your own fresh ingredients can be cheaper. Making a vegetarian pizza and having the leftover veggies used with dip the next day is making the purchase last longer than the one pre-made pizza you bought from the store.

How often do you get the craving for a juicy burger or fries from a fast-food joint? It happens to me all the time, but getting a big bag of potatoes and making the fries yourself is fun and cheap. Whether you get a fry cutter or slice up the taters by hand, you can have a lot more and pay a lot less. If you boil the oil on the stovetop or have a deep fryer, you can easily replicate the fast-food feel by taking a bit of extra time to make it yourself.

I also asked around about people's daily habits. That kick of coffee to jumpstart your morning seems to be a common trend. Fortunately I am not a coffee drinker (never had a sip in my life, actually) but that fancy four-dollar java in the morning adds up to roughly one thousand dollars per year with a stop at the store on the way to work in the morning.

With most grocery stores selling actual coffee to grind yourself, that can be a cheaper alternative to get your fix. I will admit, however, that I am addicted to fruit smoothies. Fortunately for me juice bars are popping up everywhere. I justified spending five or six bucks a drink on these things but quickly realized I knew nothing about what they were actually making me. I knew they said the fruits were in it but rarely did

I see them putting anything other than scoops of frozen stuff into the blender.

The grocery store's freezer section is a haven of frozen fruits and veggies just waiting to be blended into a homemade creation. I bought a ten-dollar blender that has two travel mugs (with lids) and a six-pound bag of mixed fruit. For the twelve-dollar bag of fruit I ended up getting nearly two weeks of morning smoothies. Like I said before, I'm not much of a cook and I used to be the type of person who would just buy it already made because it was easier. After getting beyond that reluctance, it actually became fun to create new flavors and I knew there was no sugar or gross additives in the drink and it is one-hundred percent healthy.

There is a growing number of bottled water products on store shelves. There are entire stores that sell water. Here's another admission from me: I was a water snob who insisted on having a water cooler and wouldn't drink tap water.

I would have four jugs of water delivered at a cost of just over thirty dollars. People said I was crazy but I figured I was better than them since I wasn't drinking that disgusting tap water. When I felt the financial pinch in my pocketbook my water ordering stopped and the cooler went dry.

Adding to my reassurance that tap water is OK was a visit to my parents' house. My mom offered me a bottle of water – not a brand name, just a random no-name product – and it tasted no different than tap water. At the time I told her to buy a water cooler since it was cheaper and produced less waste by not having to get rid of the little plastic bottles all the time. With a little bit of thought I realized that just because the water cooler water tasted different that didn't mean it was any better than the stuff that comes out of the tap.

I also had an idea for those empty water bottles to be reused instead of getting shipped away and recycled. After thoroughly washing them, fill them with water and keep them in the fridge. When you have company over and they ask for a bottle of water, get it for them and twist off the cap – while talking at the same time so they wouldn't notice it didn't make that new-bottle-cap-opening sound. In the case of my mom's bottled water, it could very well have been tap water just disguised in a commercial product's bottle.

You aren't really lying to your guest because you are giving them water, but it might not be the same kind they are expecting. And yes, it was Mom who taught me that with her brand-name soap in the bathroom that is just a generic refill from a giant bag squeezed into the recognizable bottle.

Know how much you are buying and prepare accordingly – meaning bring enough shopping bags and also ensuring you have enough space for everything you buy. It's happened before where my small freezer was already full and I showed up with more stuff and had to quickly eat a bunch of things just to make room in the freezer. But if you use the empty-kitchen technique where you only shop when you have no groceries, this shouldn't be a problem.

Make your list, check it twice. Bring a calculator. Smart shopping saves you money.

ONLINE SAVING

With so many people shopping online these days, you might think the days are over for clipping coupons. And maybe the physical act of cutting coupons is a thing of the past, the digital version of it is just as good.

The word "coupon" now goes by the names "promo code" or "discount code" when it comes to online shopping. A coupon is a coupon much like a discount is a discount. It's saving you money and that's the bottom line.

Back in the day you might have received coupons in the mail, now you get them in your email. You had to remember a coupon when you went to the store, now you copy and paste the info onto a webpage.

Sometimes at a store an employee is kind enough to clip a coupon for you to use if you didn't even know a discount was available. Now, when you exit a website sometimes there is a pop-up that will encourage you to keep shopping and offer you a percentage discount. Just for attempting to leave you can save twenty percent!

I made that discovery by fluke. I was shopping and accidentally clicked to close the window and I got the offer. Rather than the window closing, I clicked OK to have the discount code applied to the order I was about to place. Had I not made that mistake I would have paid full price for my order.

The key to online shopping is to fill up your cart and get to the checkout page where stores have a section for you to enter a promo code/discount code. Open up a new browser window and do a search for that store's name plus the words "promo code" and you'd be surprised how many coupon websites come up featuring offers.

Granted there are many promo codes for certain websites and not all of them will work. Some promo codes are for free shipping, a percentage off the purchase or a specified amount off a certain product. Many coupon websites will show you the frequency at which the code works (example: seventy-five percent of the time) and it might include the last time the code was tested and accepted by the store's website.

OK, so maybe it's time for me to brag a bit. Well, consider it a success story and motivation for you to be a thrifty shopper.

My initial purchase of bath products would have been twenty-four dollars but I shopped when the store offered free shipping (normally the purchase would have had an eleven-dollar shipping charge), and with a promo code I found online I applied a fifteen percent discount to the purchase. With a grand total of just over twenty dollars and savings of nearly half that amount, I'd say that was a pretty good deal considering it happened entirely by accident when I almost clicked off the website.

Despite online shopping being so popular, give me an in-store clearance rack any day. Do you really think a company will post a two-dollar discounted T-shirt on its website? It isn't even worth the web space on the page. But when you are in an actual store, look for a clearance section. At a big-box outlet's clearance store I found two T-shirts that cost me a total of four dollars.

That's right, they were marked down to three dollars each but because I used my store credit card I saved more. We aren't talking tacky and ill-fitting shirts. They were solid color and one was even a collared polo shirt. Looking at them you'd never know they were cheaper than a cup of coffee.

SAVING ADDS UP TO BIG SPENDING

"All these savings sites are costing me money." It is a quote from a message board.

With dozens of discount websites like Groupon, Deal Find and TeamBuy popping up seemingly overnight, it is becoming increasingly enticing to save online. But as one blogger wrote, all this discounting ends up having people spend more because it's deal after deal on different websites.

Everything from cookies to clothes is on the cheap, but rather than saving money, one woman spends more.

"Is anybody else buying something every day?" wrote SnglMomma in an online forum. "These deal-of-the-day things are so good that I am buying stuff just because it's cheap. I don't even eat at some of the restaurants I'm buying from yet I am loading up. I guess I'll have stuff as gifts for people."

Everybody loves a discount, we know that. But the headline "Up to ninety percent off restaurants, spas, wellness, fitness" probably doesn't help people spend less. You might save money on one purchase, but the thrill of deep discounts is a shopaholic's worst nightmare and you'll find yourself going for deal after deal.

It leads to the question: Am I really saving money on something I wouldn't have bought anyway?

Technically, yes, you are.

Sure, for twenty dollars you get a fifty-dollar credit at a store, but if you never shop at the store are you really proud of the savings? It is actually a better savings to not buy in the first place – especially if there is an expiry date for the offer and it goes unused only to waste your money.

If there happens to be a deal at a store you shop at on a regular basis or something that suits your needs the instant you see it, then there is nothing wrong with buying. It is when you are hooked into getting something just because it is discounted that could have you run into problems.

In theory, the discount websites can save you money – if you control your urges – or just stay away from them.

LITTLE PAY FOR BIG WEDDING DAY

The world buzzed when Prince William and Kate Middleton tied the knot. It had lots of women dreaming of being princesses and it had lots of men praying for a bride who doesn't expect to have an expensive princess wedding.

Either way, there's lots of ways to still have the glitz and glamor of a star-studded wedding without the cost.

Having worked at a party store for many years, I quickly learned how people can cut corners when it comes to the cost of their big day.

Wedding invitations are a couple's announcement that they are getting hitched. The embossed and fancy invites are a huge expense that can be avoided with do-it-yourself invitation paper. Rather than paying upwards of a couple thousand dollars, the bride and groom can get similar-looking invitations printed on a home computer or even at a local copy shop for a fraction of the cost.

As much as the invitation means to the couple, it doesn't always necessarily mean that much to the recipient. Evaluate the purchase because the money could be better spent elsewhere for the wedding plans.

Weddings are sometimes about tradition. Perhaps the bride's great-grandmother's dress is passed down from generation to generation. Maybe the bride wants to pay tribute to her deceased mom. A few hems and alterations could save the bride hundreds of dollars, not to mention provide a great emotional moment since the garment has a close connection to the family.

There's no question a towering wedding cake makes for beautiful pictures as the bride and groom hold the knife and pose for the ceremonious shot. There are cardboard cakes that look real and only one layer is actually cake. This is becoming increasingly popular. Taste the savings! With more and more weddings featuring buffets for guests, how many people actually have room for cake at the end of it all?

When it comes to dancing the night away, gone is the need to have a hired DJ. Talk to a friend or family member with a laptop or even an iPod to connect into a speaker system and be your own in-house music provider. Think about it: what is a DJ doing that a pre-programmed MP3 player on "shuffle" can't do?

Guests are often given a souvenir – wedding favors, they're called. Again, the instinct is to get something fancy but wedding guests often toss the giveaway into a drawer and it's never seen again. One idea is to give guests a picture CD or DVD of the wedding. It costs pennies per copy because it's a matter of burning the files once they are done and you give a memento that can feature the guests possibly making them interested in viewing it later.

There is lots of planning that goes into a wedding and while many couples opt for top-of-the-line fancy, it's more important to have a memorable day shared with loved ones to celebrate, and it shouldn't be about the superficial and expensive details.

MAKING IT MEANS MORE

Birthdays, anniversaries, Christmas: these can be expensive times for people. It's not because it costs a lot to be fancy, because that's not true. These are very commercialized events that we believe need to be costly to be fancy.

I have always been the creative type, so going to a store and buying something for the sake of buying something has never been appealing to me.

In a household of three kids, I was always the first to make something for Mother's Day or Father's Day. My brothers were quick to hit the store, grab the first funny card and appropriate gift and get out of there.

I took a bit more time (and maybe because I am cheap) but I would create a card on the computer with nice borders and graphics and a funny saying. As a kid I made a bunch of gifts for my parents because being creative was always fun to me.

Now as an adult I am the same way. I don't buy the fanciest gift or the five-dollar card that's going to get tossed out a few days later. Actually, I rarely buy cards. And come to think of it, I don't wrap gifts in expensive glossy paper.

What is the point of wowing someone with wrapping paper that's going to get torn to shreds in a few seconds anyway?

In today's world it probably implies I don't care about the person getting the gift because lack of fancy wrapping and/or a giant bow makes it seem I didn't put much effort into it. In fact, it's the total opposite: I spent a huge amount of time and little money on the gift giving.

People say "it's the thought that counts" as a sarcastic jab when someone receives a bad gift. It's too bad because the literal meaning is often true when it comes to a great gift.

Give it a shot for an upcoming holiday or event: do something creative and see the impact it makes. You might be surprised to see the reaction when you get creative and leave the impersonal stuff at the store. And, hey, saving money at the same time is a good deal.

PLAN PROPERLY TO PAY FOR PETS

As much as I love my dog, he costs me a fortune. I always say there's no cost too high that would make me consider not taking care of him anymore.

While I expected it to be a commitment like owning a car and maintaining it, I realized a dog needs its own bank account for those unexpected costs – after all, it is a member of the family.

People go to pet stores, see puppies for ridiculously expensive prices and say, I would never pay that for a dog. But people do. Taking care of it sometimes comes with the same line: I would never pay that.

But as any animal lover will tell you, the hundreds of dollars of vet bills for the unexpected illnesses or checkups, can be overwhelming. Sometimes just making an appointment at the vet can cost upwards of forty dollars. Once you are there there's the tests, exams and medication that often follow. It is not uncommon to walk out of a vet's office with two hundred dollars spent. ("That's it, no more getting sick," you probably muttered to the pooch on the way out.)

There are lots of people who opt to get pet insurance but sometimes those costs don't warrant the monthly charges you incur.

Last year I created a bank account that would be solely used for the dog. I don't put too much money into it. I have a regular monthly twenty-dollar deposit that automatically transfers to the account. You could even set one up for five dollars per week. Depending on your bank and bank accounts there might not be a charge/fee for transferring from one account to another so it's a money move you won't even notice.

When it comes closer to heart worm or annual shots time, I kick it up to thirty dollars for a few months leading up to the appointments so I'm not left strapped for money in the dog's savings account. And you might not be rich, but think of how impressive it is to say your dog has its own bank account.

Vet bills aside, there's the cost of food and toys for your pets. The belief is that expensive food is better for your pets. The bigger the brand name, the better the quality. But if you look at the nutritional information – or even just talk to the veterinarian – you'll find that a supermarket's brand might be the same and significantly cheaper.

When my dog was a puppy I was overfeeding him because he always seemed hungry and wolfed down his food very quickly. I was going through a lot of food. Despite going for walks every day, the vet said the dog needed to lose weight. The doctor gave me a plastic measuring cup that indicated how much a growing dog needs and how much an adult dog needs. Let me tell you, the dog's giant bags of food last much longer now.

As cute as dog costumes and clothes are, they really can be an unnecessary expense. It's true that a pet's feet can freeze on cold pavement in winter, but look around the house at items you already have as an alternative. If you're going to buy doggy booties, just use a couple old pairs of your socks instead.

Here's a better and safer idea: run around your home and get exercise. If you don't want to be in the cold and your pet doesn't want to be in the cold, eliminate the walk altogether. Or go for a short walk outside and come in and pick up the activity where it is warm.

All those expensive treats at the store sound so appetizing (for the dog, not me). When you look at the cost and what you are getting it makes you wonder if the price is worth it. My dog practically swallows a treat since he eats it so fast. Sure, he gets excited and sits nicely when the treat cupboard opens, but there are cheaper alternatives you can give your dog.

There's a debate about whether or not to give dogs scraps of food or leftovers from your meal. As long as it's not unhealthy foods for your dog, I don't see a problem. The trick is to not give them the food right off the counter or right off your plate. Telling the dog no when he is staring you down and licking his lips while you eat makes him go away and is then rewarded with the food. Giving him the food as his saliva is dripping on my foot while he watches me eat isn't teaching him that begging is bad.

I was one of those dog owners that gave treats for everything. Any sort of trick earned my dog a treat. Now the dog only gets a treat after he has breakfast and dinner and when I leave the house.

To make my escape, I ask him to find his special toy that gets treats loaded into it and it takes him a long time to get them out. He works his brain to figure out how to get the yummy snack while I can sneak out without him knowing. Actually, he probably wants me to leave more often so he gets more treats. But at least by the time he has spent twenty minutes working with his toy to get the reward, he will be tired out and I will be long gone.

Giving praise, play time and attention seems to be more rewarding for my dog. Sure, he loves food treats but he enjoys quality bonding time just as much. If you think about how many treats you get in a package and the amount of packages you buy in a year, you can really scale back the purchases and save lots of money.

As for toys, those little plastic squeakers can cost a lot. There should be a strategy to toy purchases. First, if you hate the squeaking sound, don't buy toys that make noise. That's a given. But if a noisy toy doesn't bother you, make your own. Take an empty drink bottle or container and bat it around the floor. Remove the plastic or paper labels so they aren't eaten and give it a few throws. Make sure you discard the toy if it gets punctured and the animal starts eating it.

When you walk down an aisle at a pet store it's interesting to see how many of the toys are actually regular items – rope, ball, etc. – but adding a pattern or design makes them a lot more expensive. I think you can imagine what my tip is for this one. Get a regular tennis ball. Use a stick from the backyard. My dog is happy playing with anything as long as he's getting my attention.

When I first got my dog I got all the fun-looking toys and paid a fortune because, I don't know, I guess I wanted to buy his love. But after a while, he quickly grew to appreciate anything I gave him because it was coming from me.

The stores sell a doggy stuffed animal for fifteen dollars but a dollar store sells the same thing for a buck. Provided the dog isn't ripping it to shreds, a stuffed doll shouldn't be a major investment. My dog brings his puppy toy to bed and falls asleep with it in his mouth. When it gets gobbed up and needs to be thrown out, I go to the closet and bring out a replacement one-dollar toy and he is just fine with it.

I also wait until after a holiday and scoop up some plush animals for half price. After Valentine's Day and all those big bears holding giant hearts are waiting for a home, I snag them and am a hero when I get home because the dog has a new friend. Once he settles down he is fast asleep holding his new pal – excuse me, his new cheap pal.

I made the mistake of buying a plush pet bed for forty dollars and after leaving him alone with it I came back into the room and saw the dog had it ripped apart in less than an hour. What does he have now? One of my old pillows on the floor and he takes care of it like it is his bed. I like to think he uses it because it has my scent so he knows it is something I personally gave him. (Whatever makes you feel better, right?)

It is just like when I moved into my house I went all out on spending but after a while you figure things out and learn how to cut corners without sacrifices.

Like owning a car, or being a homeowner, there are lots of costs that arise with being a parent to a pet. Plan ahead just like you would for having kids.

HOME SAVINGS

EVERY LITTLE BIT COUNTS

When you are living on your own with no roommates, no spouse, no one else supporting the household, it means you take control of the finances and expenses and do what you can to cut costs.

It took me a year of living in my house before I figured out tricks and tidbits to leave more money in my bank account. The first instinct when moving into a new place is to load up on furniture and fill every corner of your home. I purposely did not do this knowing I wasn't sure how my finances would work once I was on my own.

Even four years after moving into my house there are still lots of empty areas because I don't need to have a living room and a rec room and a TV in my bedroom. One friend suggested a "sitting room" in the loft area upstairs near my bedroom. It sounded great at the time but then I realized I already had a TV in the living room and sat there. It would have been an unnecessary expense.

Living with a minimalist point of view has saved me a lot of money in recent years.

I started out buying lots of groceries – even a coffee maker for when company visits – yet quickly scaled back when I got a little out of hand with my ambitious purchases. I don't drink coffee, I rarely have people over and the coffee maker has sat in its box since I bought it before moving into my house – yes, four years ago.

We hear that devices with a clock – TV, computer, microwave, etc. – use more energy when in standby mode and not in actual operation. Taking that to heart (and to the extreme, according to some) I unplug the microwave since I use it maybe one time in a month. My computer is unplugged when I am not at home and every night when I go to bed. On a weekend I have nothing plugged in in my home office.

In the living room I have two floor lamps. Each acts as a decoration because neither is plugged in. That's right, they are fully functional but don't give light since the cords aren't connected to anything. In the summer when it stays bright until nearly ten o'clock in the evening there is no need to have a lamp when I go to bed before it even gets dark. In the winter, it is dark early but the brightness from the TV illuminates the room so it helps with the lighting situation.

In the cold winter, people have the heat cranked all day. Whether they are there or not, homeowners keep the place toasty warm for their arrival. Electronic thermostats can be programmed to leave the house cool when you aren't around and crank up the heat moments before you arrive. Rather than having a furnace run all day for the comfort of nobody, you will save money only having the place heated when you need it.

When I bought my house I was on a budget program because of the unpredictable cold prairie winter. I paid the same amount every month and in the summer it would balance out so I either had a credit in my account or would have to make a payment to get caught up with the actual hydro usage. It has always ended up being a credit for me.

The problem with the averaging program was the first year my monthly amount was based on the previous owner's twelve months. It worked out to be two hundred per month that I paid for electricity and heat in my house. I was able to bring it down to one-hundred-sixty dollars the next year by using less every month which lowered the average monthly consumption. The next year it was down to one-hundred-thirty-five dollars per month when I discovered the programmable thermostat would only be heating the house between five o'clock in the afternoon and ten o'clock in the evening. Otherwise I wasn't home or I was sleeping.

Most people have a temperature preference when they sleep. Some like it hot, some like it cold. If you like it hot, get a fuzzy velour blanket (or two). Also, if you have pets, cuddle up against them. A natural fur coat is something to be appreciated on a cold winter night.

Another cheap alternative to staying warm is to get a hot water bottle. If you are quick to fall asleep like I am, place the bottle on your chest or feet and the water will stay warm enough until you doze off. Factoring in what it costs to fill a hot water bottle compared to running a furnace all night, you'll quickly see the savings if you adjust your heat source.

Saving water was a tough one for me. I love my baths. I can spend hours in the bathtub, refilling it every twenty minutes to have it as hot as possible. I offset that water usage by rarely washing dishes (if it's just me in the house, how much water is it to wash one plate and one set of cutlery) or filling the sink once and going through all the plates in the cupboard before giving them all a good wash.

My house doesn't have a low-flush toilet. It's still an old clunker that is designed to figuratively flush your money down the drain. But rather than having a full toilet tank, I have containers filled with sand taking up space in the tank. This prevents the entire tank from filling up with water on a flush and greatly cuts down on the usage. A gallon here and a gallon there will make a difference on your next water bill.

PAY LESS FOR YOUR PHONE

If you are like most North Americans, you probably pay more for a phone than some of your utilities. We'll get to cellphone costs in a minute.

A common complaint is an expensive cable bill. That could also include your Internet and phone service. While we once wanted every possible feature to keep with the times, it is cheaper to strip down your service and go with the minimums you require.

If you don't make long distance calls, why pay for the full phone service? Don't need call waiting or a digital answering machine? Get rid of 'em and don't pay for them. Ridding yourself of useless features could cut your bill in half.

Get this: my parents were renting a phone from the phone company. Back in the day you rented a phone for five dollars per month and when most people got with the times (in the nineties) my parents were still shelling out sixty dollars per year – for over thirty years. That is one mighty expensive phone! They only recently went to the store and got a twenty-dollar cordless phone.

Let's tackle the dreaded cellphone bill. First off, after that long story about landlines, you might already be wondering why you have that and a cellphone. Well, you just reduced your expenses by deciding to get rid of one! Chances are it will be the "home phone" since it is more convenient to run around with a mobile device.

And as convenient as a cellphone is, the costs can be ridiculous. When BlackBerrys first came out one of my colleagues had one and his bill was about ninety dollars per month. I thought it was outrageous. Was it really necessary to pay more than double what I was for a "regular" cellphone?

Whenever my bill came I purposely avoided looking at it. There were pages and pages of calls, there's a break down of minutes, data usage, charges, credits and you almost needed a math degree to understand it.

Upon closer examination when I thought the amount owing seemed high one month, I actually tackled the pluses and minuses and found I was being charged incorrectly.

When I called customer service to discuss the problem with a representative, he informed me my price plan was fairly old and that the current features I had were cheaper and I got more for the price.

I was going over my monthly data limit only to get charged for the overage. The rep told me the new data plan was five dollars cheaper and I got more than twice what I had at the time. How many months did I get dinged only to have someone on the inside be nice enough to point out that little detail?

Also during the call – and I'm sure the guy's boss probably wouldn't have appreciated the employee pointing this out – but knowing my phone has Wi-fi capabilities, I was using data more than I should have. He told me a common mistake people make is using a cellphone for its web surfing and data but don't take into consideration the wireless network at home.

Chances are the Wi-fi at home is faster than the mobile service, anyway. Turning off the feature on your phone and connecting to a wireless network nearly eliminates the need for a data plan in the first place.

I realize more people use their cellphone while out and about and Wi-fi isn't available everywhere, but if you spend a lot of time at home, at school or even work, find out about tapping into Wi-fi networks wherever you go.

If you work in an office but constantly check Facebook and Twitter on your phone – and you know the company doesn't mind – either use your work computer or connect your phone on the company's Wi-fi network.

If you assess the amount of time you will be using your smartphone to surf the web, you might be able to keep a minimal data plan and change your connection as needed.

Some mobile companies have taken "data" one step further – perhaps clever marketing to think you're getting something you're not – but they offer "social media" data plans and that allegedly is perfect for the person who can't stay off Facebook- and Twitter-type sites.

My question is: Is there really a difference in data or is "social media data" just data dressed up. It is worth checking out to compare the price of data and social media data. You could be getting scammed or paying more for less.

Sure, the billing phone call lasted about an hour, but it ended with me removing phone features I was paying for that I never used and it reduced my bill by about twenty dollars per month, giving me more of what I needed than what I had before dialing in.

As for being overcharged, it wasn't a matter of just having them stop the incorrect billing, I had them look through my account and see when it all started.

Despite the cellphone company offering to credit my account for the overpayments, I demanded an actual refund to my credit card. It's great they had no problem taking more money from me than they should have and I wasn't going to settle for simply a credit to my mobile account.

How else can you reduce your phone bill? I know it is tempting to email and post pictures while you are on vacation, but find out for sure the long distance and roaming charges for your plan. Sometimes if you are in the same country there isn't an added cost, but depending on the plan you might incur extra charges.

Some people suggest getting a calling card and using that to log on and connect with people, but if you are away for a vacation, don't be a loser who is attached at the hip (literally) to your phone. Live in the moment and enjoy the day. Forget about being a Facebook nerd and Twitter geek for a few days. You might not believe me, but life goes on!

The thing I look forward to most when I travel is the excuse of high roaming charges to make me shut off my cellphone. I will admit the first hour or two when I land in another country I have the urge to check email and text people. But it is quite freeing to be in a tropical locale and know your cellphone isn't distracting you all day.

If you really need to check in while you are away, find a coffee shop or Internet café that offers cheap or free Internet connectivity. If you must check in with the online world, use Wi-fi and you might not even have to pay a penny to get your Facebook fix. But for the sake of your cellphone bill: turn off the signal so your phone isn't constantly downloading information and quietly adding dollars to your bill.

Remember, what you do when you are away will take a month to catch up with you and you don't want the happy memory from your trip to be overshadowed by the crazy phone bill.

Take it from me – I had a two-thousand-dollar bill when I came back from my first vacation and that is the one memory I have. I was glued to my phone and had to constantly check in with everyone that I ruined the trip.

EXTRA COVERAGE SAVES THE DAY

When I bought my house I was offered a free home warranty for one year. That's not to be confused with the insurance that I had. The warranty covered things like a hot water tank, furnace or central air conditioning breakdown.

My attitude was, It's free for a year, so why not? When the one year had run its course I debated whether or not to pay the thirteen dollars per month for the continued coverage. I kept it going and it paid off a few months later.

The furnace was acting up and later stopped working. That's right: dead of winter, no heat. I immediately called the hydro company to have the problem fixed. I didn't realize I should have called the toll-free number for the warranty company and they would have sent out an expert, bypassing the hydro company altogether.

The hydro company sent someone to check out the problem and it turned out the furnace needed a repair. I had to pay for the part and the charge was added to my monthly bill.

After it was all done, I remembered my warranty information and called the company to see what the next step was. I was told I should have called them first and they would have dispatched someone to check out the problem. In taking the wrong steps I could have forfeited any reimbursement of costs because I didn't follow the proper procedure.

My reasoning was it was nearly forty degrees below zero and I was in a panic when I woke up to a freezing house. I played the sympathy card but it was an entirely true story.

I had to submit the work order information from the hydro company. The adjusters reviewed the information, but, again, I was reminded I might not get approved.

There was a fifty-dollar deductible and the furnace part cost about one-hundred-twenty dollars.

Weeks later a check arrived (less the deductible) and my warranty came in handy.

Not even two years later there was a similar problem with my central air conditioning. It was a sweltering hot day when I came home only to find the A/C was running but no cold air was coming out of the vents. In this instance I did the right thing and called the warranty company, they dispatched a specialist to come to my house and fix the problem and I was once again feeling cool.

I had to personally pay upfront the heating and air conditioning company because it was an emergency, but had I been able to wait until a weekday, the warranty company would have handled the payment and I would have just been billed the fifty-dollar deductible.

Sometimes it pays to get the extra add-ons when it comes to keeping an eye on your property.

VIEWS ABOUT GETTING USED

Wanting a new computer is one thing, needing a new computer is another.

Like most people I want the latest, the fastest, the coolest, the amazing-est – you get the picture. But I dread making the switch because it means starting all over with the settings and setup that has taken years of OCDish tendencies to get just right.

The mere thought of the word "refurbished" makes people shut down immediately. People associate refurbished electronics with being used and old and gross. That isn't always the case.

There are plenty of discount computer resellers that fix up old computers and modernize them to be very much comparable to what you would get in big-box stores.

Finding somebody who works closely with customers and provides personal and customized service can also be a ticket to scoring big with a new computer.

Think about it: a person who takes in old computers and fixes them up has lots of extra parts kicking around that can be installed to tailor a new machine for you.

Don't plan on gaming or surfing? Why pay for a top-of-the-line model that showcases those features?

Whether you go to a store or find someone who pieces together computers, there is a simple question to ask yourself: What am I going to do with the computer?

Give the tech your list of needs and you can get a custom machine built just for you. Don't get an out-of-the-box computer that will have you clueless about half its features. Of course it sounds great in the store when they can ramble about the gigas-of-this and megas-of-that but ask what that means for your use.

Chances are the small-business owner isn't going to screw you over because he or she needs your repeat business and your referrals. There's a better chance they will take care of you than a store where you're one of hundreds going through every day.

Pick and choose your features to get a customized machine and it could be much cheaper and a better experience in the long run.

As always: do your shopping homework!

MUST YOU LIVE THERE?

I fully understand that people sometimes have little choice about where they live. Whether that is because of family or financial constraints, these can be major factors in where we reside.

But are you living within your means? I'm not talking about reckless spending on a car you don't need, I'm talking about the place you live.

Even before the selection process begins, it is vital your current financial status is examined. This could be with the help of an accountant, mortgage broker or sitting and crunching numbers on your own. My first move was planned a year before I actually packed up and set up shop in a new place. I had been stashing away money for twelve months and had ten thousand dollars saved up before I even considered looking at properties. Then and only then (with much trepidation) did I begin my search.

But the monthly mortgage or rent payments played a big role in my decision making. What could I afford and was it realistic to say I could sustain the costs for months and years?

When I was shopping for my first home after leaving my parents' nest, I naturally wanted a house. An apartment would never be mine. My brothers tried to convince me to buy a condo but in the end having to pay monthly condo fees seemed too much like rent. The property would technically belong to me but upgrading windows or the roof almost needed a plea to a panel of people to get approval.

There was a lot of consideration into where I would move. I wanted the freedom of owning but also didn't want the responsibility of yard upkeep. I had never cut grass before, never really shoveled snow and had no interest in either of those two homeowner duties.

My brothers did what they could to discourage me from getting a house and to move into a condo, highlighting that yard maintenance is taken care of through the monthly condo fees I didn't want to pay. It had me wonder and calculate how much it would be worth to have someone do that work for me. I still couldn't get over the idea of paying an extra charge to live in my own place. So, a condo was out.

For a brief time I considered an apartment. I wouldn't be responsible for snow or grass or even fixing appliances that break down. Seemed like a sweet deal. But in crunching some numbers that the rent would be more than the mortgage of a decent house, it was still an undesirable situation.

Picking a home is not like getting a pet – which is also one of the points to consider: do you want pets? – so you have to think ahead because, as people say, a house is the biggest purchase most people will ever make.

I knew there were no kids in my future. I wanted pets. I wanted a yard (but not the responsibility of it). I wanted to own the property. I wanted to have a say in what would happen to it. For me, a house was the most desirable choice.

House selection is something that should be considered a little more extensively than, "Oh, it's so nice inside, I want it." The first thing people do when they go into a house is look around. They look up, they look down. Prior to the visit had they thought of how much space they actually need? Is it in a neighborhood that is going to complement their lifestyle? We always hear "it's in such a nice area" but does that mean it is convenient for work or school or having kids?

Location, location, location. If you take public transportation and don't mind living far away from the places you need, then go for it. I wanted to be central and within walking distance to the major staples – work, shopping, family.

If you live in the south end and work in the west end and need to pick up the kids from daycare in the north end, you might find yourself getting really impatient in a bus (not to mention spending so much time commuting every day).

Once you've found a perfect area, the next thing to consider is what you can and can't live with. For me all I needed was the basics: one bedroom, a living room, a kitchen and a bathroom. Instead I got a basement, main floor, upstairs, three bedrooms and big front and backyard but I took into consideration the price, size and features of other houses in the neighborhood.

With just me living in the house I wouldn't have the expenses that a family of four would. I wouldn't have lights on all over the house. I wouldn't have water usage skyrocketing because everybody has to shower. I wouldn't have furnace vents open throughout the house since I didn't have to heat most of the rooms in the winter.

Having so much extra space in my house led to the discussion about renting out and having roommates. It definitely would have been a consideration if I was struggling to make ends meet, but since I was financially stable I didn't consider having people live under my roof.

But factoring in the cost of rent and what people would be paying for a bachelor apartment, I could have easily rented out two bedrooms and the basement and had three tenants. That would have boosted my income, had the yard chores taken care of and made the housework a lot easier. Maybe I should rethink this!

SAVING DINING DOLLARS

Whether there is a special occasion or you are just too lazy to cook, everybody loves a good meal out. The good meal out often leads to an expensive bill in the end. There are some obvious things you can do to keep it a cheap dining experience, while other tips need some creativity.

First and foremost: order water. As restaurants often offer free refills on soft drinks and coffee, the cost of these menu items has increased. It is not uncommon to pay nearly three dollars for a watered down fountain drink. Getting a glass of water is free (if it isn't, you might want to rethink your restaurant choice) and it balances out the flavor overload you'll be having with the meal.

As a teenager I had a job at a restaurant and had no idea what an appetizer was. Growing up, my family only ever went to fast-food restaurants and the meal was the meal. We didn't have any extras, certainly never dessert because we ate enough to keep us full.

My dining habits are very much the same now. I will only have the main course and I save a lot with no salad, no appetizer, no dessert and no beverage.

If you have a family and the kids probably won't eat their entire meal or will fuss with what's given to them, you can pull a switcheroo to trick, uh, convince them they are getting a really good meal. And the answer is simple. Have the server tell the kitchen staff to put some of your food on an empty plate as a kid's meal. This way you can tell the little ones they are having the exact same thing as you and that it tastes great. Rather than paying full price for a meal that might end up on the table or floor, you can save money by giving a little bit of your portion to your hungry rugrat.

If all else fails, bring a small bag of food the youngster picked out before getting to the restaurant. Have him or her choose their meal/treat and bring it to the restaurant. This way there is no complaining they don't want it because they picked it out. Most restaurants are cool with you bringing something for kids to eat if they are under a certain age.

There are two great sections of a menu that I love ordering from: kids menu and seniors menu. As a teen I quickly flipped away from those pages thinking I couldn't order from them. But I was pleasantly surprised when a chicken dinner on the seniors menu was not only cheaper than the main course in the regular section of the menu but it was actually the meal I wanted. There was fine print at the bottom of the page saying non-seniors would be charged an extra dollar for ordering off that menu.

Over at fast-food restaurants it is easy to get hooked on the extras. You can get cheese with that, bacon with that, gravy with that and these extras can end up adding a few extra dollars to the bill that should really only be a few dollars, anyway.

Getting the burger combo is five dollars but when you add this and that your meal nearly doubles in price. Back to basics with how you order your food. And in the long run, the more greasy ingredients the more unhealthy the meal becomes, so you are doing yourself a favor by skimping on the extras.

Not that I am suggesting you loot restaurants of their condiments, but oftentimes you get thrown a handful of ketchup or vinegar with your meal. Keep them! If you don't use the condiments during that meal, take them with you for another meal. Use them at home. I threw them out with the empty wrappers and containers from the meal but it saves you in the long run by keeping a collection of them at home. This is especially true if you don't normally use the condiment very often and only need a little bit instead of having a full jar or container go to waste.

I can't say it enough: coupons, coupons, coupons. Save them for a rainy day. There is nothing wrong with using a coupon for a night out. Who cares if you might be considered a cheap date. Flip around that criticism and tell people you are a financial expert and have money for the best things in life – not just for food.

Many people give couples a gift card to a restaurant. Whether it is an anniversary present, a wedding gift or a thank-you gesture, sometimes playing a card game works in your favor – and by card game, I mean a gift card game.

Swapping gift cards from one restaurant that might not be your favorite for a dining establishment you enjoy frequenting is a good way to get some use out of a gift. You can find someone to trade or even use a swapping service online.

Doing this will ensure no cards are wasted and you end up getting a free meal when you go out.

SEASONAL SAVINGS

GIVE YOURSELF A SPRING BREAK

With the kids on spring break there's going to be lots of time to fill. A whole week of energetic children wanting to do as much as they can until school starts again. But if you are on a budget, finding activities for the youngsters might seem like a daunting task.

Here are some ideas to make sure spring break doesn't make you go broke.

For most parents, work isn't an option. Work has to be done. This might mean sending the kids to a babysitter or even more frightening: leaving them home alone. Either way, have a scheduled plan mapped out to ensure the week goes smoothly (and cheaply).

Contact neighbors and see if anyone is taking their kids to a community center for an afternoon of activities. Often there are drop-in opportunities that cost next to nothing, if not free. Not only will this burn some energy, it will give the kids their exercise for the day.

Maybe get a group of kids together to come up with a dance routine. If someone has a camera phone or camcorder, make a music video and have the gang dress up and create a storyline for the video. If they are old enough, perhaps introduce a basic video-editing program to complete the final project. (Yes, there are free programs out there!) And if you approve of getting screen time, YouTube surfers love cute videos of kids. And with the Internet, who knows where your talent will be discovered and which talk show or celebrity will give the group a platform to launch them into superstardom. Hey, you've heard of Justin Bieber, right?

Create activities around the house. Put together a scavenger hunt of household items. Create a list of clues to the secret items and put a sticker on the bottom or back of each one so the kids know when they found the right item. You can even put letters on them to spell out a secret word (maybe the family's last name or the pet's name).

Gathering up old newspapers and magazines for a word game is an exciting idea. Flip through some pages and make note of items in pictures – a tree, balloons, etc. – and have the kids go through the stack of publications to look for the items. Perhaps tape coupons to the pages good for a free cookie, Slurpee, or extra TV time as encouragement.

As much as parents want the kids to stay off the computer, it can also be a creative distraction. Use a drawing program to create a family logo or welcome sign for the house. You can also make a list of family member's birthdays, anniversaries and dates of holidays and assign the kids to create greeting cards or signs for each occasion. Not only is this cheaper than going to a store to buy decorations, it encourages creativity.

Depending on the age of the children, there are always animal shelters, senior's homes and charities looking for volunteers.

Inquire about opportunities to have the kids give back to the community and help out those needing a hand. This will also teach them an important life lesson about being an outstanding citizen in the neighborhood (and it looks great on a resumé).

After volunteering, kids might look forward to a good spring cleaning to donate old clothes or toys to area organizations. Talk about killing two birds with one stone!

The important thing to keep in mind is creativity doesn't have to cost much. Sometimes it is the unconventional activities that are more fun. You'd be surprised how much more kids appreciate the activities when they know parents did all the planning to make them feel special.

MAKE IT THE MOST WONDERFUL TIME OF THE YEAR!

Parents and kids are both counting down the days until school is back after summer break – parents perhaps with excitement and kids with dread. But back-to-school shopping can be fun for both: kids can get the latest school gear and parents can use some comparative shopping skills to save money.

With so many stores competing for your back-to-school bucks, you can often find great deals everywhere. But if you dig a little deeper (and use some creativity), you can often find great deals.

The mailbox is filling up with flyers but the Internet is a great tool for getting better bargains.

Earlier I mentioned there are lots of websites that offer lists of "promo codes" – read that as online coupons – and when you complete your purchase online you can add a promo code. This is often something of a discount or free shipping depending on the store and its offer.

Take for instance a big-ticket item like a scientific calculator. You might see one in a flyer for forty dollars and a sale price of thirty dollars. But online you can do a search for the store and the words "promo code" and you might find that you can save fifteen percent on your entire purchase. And maybe you get lucky because the store is offering free shipping that weekend, too.

Double bonus! Not only did you save on shipping, you got a discount on an already sale-priced item.

Another tip is to scope out the school year because not all supplies will be needed on day one. You might be able to pick up certain items at a discount during the "off season" when they get marked down. If one course or class isn't happening until the second semester, is it necessary to buy supplies for it now?

Buying in multiples can save you money. The "two for" deals might seem unnecessary now, but if you have a youngster heading to school in a couple years, buy now and save that second set of items. Keep a closet of supplies and the savings will add up especially if you find a great back-to-school deal.

By being a savvy shopper not only can kids follow the coolest trends, the parents stay cool by not going broke!

HALLOWEEN COSTS ARE SCARY

Something scarier than Halloween costumes is the price of them. It seems that you have to save up just to get the actual outfit, much less the accessories to go with it to complete the look.

It's true that the expensive costumes from a store are impressive and will catch people's attention, but sometimes the creativity of making your own is funnier, but more importantly, more fun.

I'm not suggesting you grab items from around the house to put together a lame costume. Well, I guess you can if you want. But half the fun in getting ready for Halloween is the planning and, if you're like me, seeing how you can make it work for little money.

Thinking about what's popular this year: let's say Jersey Shore. On some costume store websites you can get a costume for about forty dollars. If you're like me you might think that doesn't sound like much initially but if you do some creative thinking you can make the outfit for about nine dollars.

It is not hard to find muscle shirts and slinky black dresses at a thrift store. In fact, a dress for two dollars is not unheard of at many stores. It is tacky, it is short, it does the trick. And you have to have the shoes to go with the outfit. Guess what, fifty cents for a pair of heels at the thrift store. Remember, the joke of dressing like a Jersey Shore character is to look ridiculous.

So the dress is bought. Next, you need the hair. You'd be surprised how easy (and cheap) it is to spray paint your hair and stick an empty soup can underneath it to give it that "poof." You could go out and buy the official Jersey Shore wig for fifteen dollars, but a two-dollar bottle of hairspray paint and an empty can from the recycling bin is way more economical.

To complete the look, many people opt for orange face paint to exaggerate the tans of the MTV cast. A quick trip to the dollar store can score you a one-dollar tube of face paint. Also, getting ridiculous sunglasses (the bigger the better) will seal the deal and make you look like a Jersey Shore star.

As for the kids, they will naturally want the expensive costumes of the trendy characters that are out now. Like I mentioned before, part of the fun with Halloween is the planning and involvement to make your own customized costume. It won't take much convincing to have the kids agree to start from scratch and have a good time picking out all the details of their own costume.

"Let's make it something special like nobody else has," you could say. "Everybody is going to be wearing the one from the store so let's make our own."

This is where trips to discount stores and craft shops will come in handy and save you a bundle.

Buying some material or construction paper or even just getting ideas walking up and down the aisles of the stores will help. When Prince William and Kate's royal wedding happened, I was on a mission to create a hilarious hat to watch the ceremony. I had a goal and accomplished it by putting in a little time and effort.

So you've completed your look for Halloween, but how are you dressing up your home? Years ago when I worked at a party supply store, people were coming in and spending hundreds of dollars for decorations to have the flashiest house on the block. And that's great if it's a passion of theirs to create a spectacular spectacle, but let's be realistic: is it necessary to go overboard like that? It really isn't.

I am a firm believer that dollar stores should be ransacked when it comes to holiday decorating. There were many decorations our party store sold for fifteen dollars that you can get for a buck or two at a discount store. Don't get me wrong, the quality might not be as good, but if it is simply a decoration that is going to hang on a wall or outside for one day of the year, durability shouldn't be an issue. Even if it is, at two dollars to replace it, you're not all that bad off.

Many stores sell decorations at inflated prices. For instance, glow-in-the-dark products are generally available all year round. Just putting those products in a Halloween section can see the price skyrocket. How do I know? I was one of the employees that had to move them there and mark up the price.

Black-light bulbs and other types of lighting are not specifically a Halloween product. If you buy some earlier in the year you might be able to get them cheaper. The party store I managed was great at remerchandising products to tie them in with different events.

Like costumes, decorations take planning. Thankfully I had stockpiled decorations after my employment at the party store, but take into consideration what and where you are decorating before you go crazy and overspend. I made that mistake by getting even more stuff when I moved into a bigger house. All I was decorating was the front window (that is almost entirely hidden by a big tree) and the front doorway.

I rushed out to get more things but when it came time to set up I had stuff in packages that I had no use for.

Halloween is one of those tricky decorating times because unless you are hosting a party or having people over for a Halloween-related event, you don't need to dress up a large area of your home. For me, it was all about the visuals as people went by and then when the kids spent that five seconds getting the candy before rushing off.

I had previously bought a strobe light and fog machine but as I fumbled with holding open the door, giving kids candy and making sure I wasn't forgetting anybody, the last thing on my mind was the wow factor of a blast of fog for the kids. Depending on where you live, you might even have troubles with your windows fogging up as the cool fall air mixed with the indoor heat makes a mess of any sort of window decorations you have.

Sometimes less is more with decorating. You have to remember Halloween isn't a "season" so overdoing it like you would for Christmas might not be the smartest financial decision. For the most part, Halloween is completely forgotten about the next day. Actually, I took a lesson from my mom who sets up Halloween decorations the day of and takes them down when she shuts off the front light and calls it a night once the trick-or-treaters have gone.

The key to a great Halloween is keeping the costs down and the creativity up.

DECK THE HALLS AND TRIM THE COSTS, IT'S CHRISTMAS

It is one of the most expensive times of year for me. I can only imagine what it costs a family with kids. Let me do my best to offer up some ways to cut costs of what is a magical but expensive time of year.

Christmas is tricky since it often encompasses a month of dinners, get-togethers, decorating and gift giving. (I feel poorer just listing those things.) So what can be done?

When it comes to dinners, opt for homemade meals. It's too easy to have a function catered or even order in but the cost can be outrageous if you are entertaining a large group. Suggest a potluck-style meal where people bring something for everybody and you could actually get out of having to make food if you are hosting. I am not suggesting be a Scrooge, but there is something to be said for a host who has had to coordinate the event and make sure it runs smoothly in their own home.

If you are responsible for making a dish and bringing it to a party, pick something you like. If you are going home with leftovers (you can also opt for something that won't spoil quickly) you might as well have something you like rather than getting home and throwing out the crusty bland leftovers.

At the same time, if you are bringing a salad, only make a little bit with dressing and mix more as needed, this way you won't have a half bowl of soggy mess to dump out at the end of the night. You can go home with a bag of crisp lettuce ready to use the next day (or for your next Christmas party!).

Oftentimes a Christmas party might require somebody to bring the munchies or the soft drinks. The thing to remember is to not put it all out right away. This will only encourage people to be gluttons and eat way more than they need to. The munchies are simply to tide you over until the actual meal comes out. People often eat more because there is a giant full bowl in front of them. Pacing the food presentation could save you food and, in turn, money.

I have gone to a Christmas dinner where someone served a bucket of chicken from a local restaurant instead of cooking up a bird for the meal. Perhaps it was taking the easy (and really greasy way out) but looking at the costs of a bucket of chicken to feed a group of twenty people, you're better off buying two small chickens and actually cooking them yourself.

While I understand people get busy during the holidays, finances are something to keep in mind all year. It is a delicate balance of cutting corners and looking cheap at Christmas or doing something meaningful for the people with whom you will be spending the holiday.

I can tell you that there was a lot of whispering and murmuring when the buckets of chicken were put on the dinner table, but the complaints weren't about the actual food but that the non-chef took the easy way out. The bucket bringer clearly wasn't concerned about saving money during the holidays.

Leftovers are a great thing. One meal can last two or three days. Don't be embarrassed about bringing to-go containers to pack up some food to take with you. Sure, this might sound contradictory to my previous advice about wanting to skimp on the amount of food you put out or bring, but when there is food that has been prepared and needs to be eaten or taken, take it!

We groan that we'll never eat mashed potatoes or stuffing again but when it is a deciding factor about buying groceries or eating out, you might appreciate the leftover holiday meal and it saving you a few dinner dollars.

OK, there is more to Christmas than food. And if you are not a cook (like me) you can sometimes get out of bringing a contribution to the meal by offering to bring some decorations and décor. People know I am not a cook and often suggest I bring something that doesn't need to be prepared. Many of them realize I have a stockpile of holiday decorations from my time as a party store manager and I am asked to bring some items to create a festive feel. There is nothing wrong with taking some of your decorations from home and bringing them to a loved one's party and then putting them back up at your place once their party is over. Seriously, it sounds cheap but nobody will notice.

The dreaded gift exchange. Sigh. Whether it is with co-workers at the office or a group of friends having a Christmas party, you don't want to look like a Grinch by not participating, but you also don't want to waste money buying something for someone you don't really know or don't care about.

If you are a hobbyist and make items at home, use one or two of them as your contribution for the Secret Santa exchange. Remember, most people are buying a generic gift because you don't know who the recipient will be. It could be the boss, it could be the chatty office receptionist or the guy who always looks miserable. There is no way to strike out because people don't have high expectations for this type of gift exchange.

There is also the idea of re-gifting and re-wrapping something you received but don't want and giving it to someone else. Sure, it is tacky but it's also not wasteful. It doesn't take much encouragement to convince yourself that it is OK to give something you have no use for, anyway. While that doesn't mean you give it to someone because you don't care about them and it is the easy way out, it does give you a reason to reuse something you otherwise wouldn't keep for yourself.

One of the most expensive sides to Christmas is the gifts. There is no hiding that fact. Growing up our family had a thirty-dollar limit for presents for each person. As a kid it didn't seem too much since I just bought for my parents and my two brothers. But now that everybody is older (and married with kids), that brings the total to ten people, not including the names of relatives I draw in the extended family gift exchange.

As you feel your wallet emptying you wonder how you are going to take care of everybody and not go broke. This is where your powers of persuasion come in.

It is easy to spend without questioning where and why your dollars are going where they are. I was buying gifts for every family member but on the receiving (spending) end, I was only getting one gift from my brother and his wife. Doing some math that meant I was paying sixty dollars for the two of them while they only spent thirty on me.

It didn't take much convincing to get out of having to buy for two of them when a thirty-dollar gift card to a restaurant worked just as nicely for the couple to spend a night out together. (Partner that with guilting grandma and grandpa into babysitting that night and you really got off easy.)

Next up is the nieces and nephews. You can't be a good aunt or uncle and not get the kids anything. What's the next best thing? Making a basket of educational materials.

Yes, I sound like a cheapskate but I would much rather work on a gift basket of learning tools than on toys that will keep the kids entertained until the next toy is opened.

I have long been a believer in buying youngsters fun but educational gifts. It is also when I run to a dollar or discount store and load up on construction paper, markers, paints and other supplies to encourage creativity. I have also found stencils online to print out and collate to make a coloring book. It's true, a little resourcefulness can prevent you from wasting money on an expensive book when you can make one for much cheaper.

Another coloring book idea is taking family photos and digitally editing them and using special treatments to strip down a picture to be black and white or stenciled. Again, this is cheaper but it's also more personal than simply coloring generic images.

For kids that are a little bit older, rather than buying presents, make a coupon to spend the afternoon together. Take a trip to the mall or go see a movie and instead of spending sixty bucks on presents for two kids, you can create memories for cheap and have a good time in the process.

What happens with the cousin whose name you drew in the family gift exchange? Oftentimes it is secret who picked whom, but in our family there are only a few people you can pick. The rule is we can't have someone in our immediate family we already buy for. Mathematically it ends up working out I will buy for a cousin since my brothers, sisters-in-law and parents are excluded from the names I can get.

Back to your negotiation and persuasion skills because sometimes you can wheel and deal and get a different name than the one you picked. Think about it: you aren't close with the relative you selected but you know someone else is. Play the game of making a deal and you can trade to get a relative you know really well.

If you play your cards right you could end up with the person who picked your name. That's a perfect scenario because you can easily say, "Hey, I don't need anything for Christmas, do you? No? OK, let's just do a lunch together and call it even." More often than not that's the easiest and cheapest way to eliminate buying one more present for the holidays.

After the gifts have been exchanged and your home is full of stuff you don't have room for there's a couple decisions to make. One: what do you keep? And, two: where do you put it?

A solution would be to donate any of the items you don't want. Whether it is ill-fitting clothing that you can't return or a duplicate of something you already have, you could find a way to have a charity benefit. Another use would be to re-gift as mentioned earlier in this chapter. But you can always sell items online. You can make money from Christmas gifts.

You would be selling a brand-new item that could probably fetch you the suggested retail price. That's sheer profit from receiving a gift and having no use for it. With so many online auction and marketplace sites, it wouldn't be hard for you to find an interested buyer.

So, you saved money (and possibly made money) on gifts and food, but how about the decorations? Unlike Halloween, Christmas decorations are often up for much of December and early into the new year. The mistake I made the first year I was living in my own house was that I overbought and could decorate the entire house with all the extra stuff. Talk about a waste of money.

It is easy to get lost in the beauty of ornaments but there can be too much of a good thing. Every year I seem to have more decorations than I can fit on my Christmas tree. I buy some, I get some as gifts and pretty soon I will need a bigger tree.

Clever staff at a store will merchandise the expensive patterned tableware right in the middle of the Christmas section. The plates and napkins have cute Santas and reindeer but they are probably twice as much as a solid color set. Think about the cost of a napkin that will be used to wipe a mouth and get thrown out moments later. Is it worth the price you pay?

Getting solid red- or green-colored napkins and plates is not only cheap but people automatically associate the colors with the holiday so it is just as good for spreading the holiday cheer. When it comes to decorations, basic colors are also the way to go. Depending on which home or decorating publications you read, you often hear that solid colors and basics is the most appealing to the eye.

I used to like the crazy blinking and flashing strings of lights that had eight settings where you're bound to have a seizure if you stared at them too long. I was told by a retail merchandiser that the rapid changing of colors and flashes is distracting when people watch TV and those with the crazy lights often unplug them since they are a nuisance. It's one of those seemed-like-a-good-idea-at-the-time purchases.

After learning the lesson that I reluctantly accepted, it was noticeable to me when I went to stores or someone's house and they had the strobe-like lights in the window or on the tree. It really is tacky and distracting. Now I opt for solid colors that don't flash or blink and those strings of lights are usually a cheaper buy than the crazy ones that do tricks.

By now I sound like a do-it-yourself guru, but when you think about the cost savings, it really is the way to go when it comes to decorating.

If you think about the cost of ink and paper for your printer, you can pretty much print out images and patterns at home and make your own decorations. Find some pictures of snowmen or elves and make your own holiday scene for the wall or front window. Get some clear lights and illuminate your work of art. Who knows, you might create a setting more famous than the nativity scene. OK, maybe not, but think big when making a display.

Again, if there are kids at home, this could be an easy way to get crafty and decorate the house at the same time. Encourage the kids to use creativity and items around the house to come up with a holiday scene for the neighborhood to enjoy. Kids take great pride in being able to show something they made so it won't take much convincing to get them to participate.

REALISTIC NEW YEAR'S RESOLUTIONS

You've heard them, you've made them, but have you kept them? New year's resolutions are a great idea in theory after gorging during the holiday season when the pants get a little tighter, but is it necessary to set up false hope by promising to make a change when the calendar flips to a new year?

There are generally two resolutions made: stop smoking and eat better/get in shape. People argue that both of these feats should be a gradual lifestyle change and not happen immediately. We hear quitting smoking is tough to do. People gradually cut back in the hopes of wiping out entirely the unhealthy habit.

Same goes for working out and getting in shape. People say it is unrealistic and dangerous to go from couch potato to gym rat without easing into the transition.

How about saving money? Some people who still make easy-to-break resolutions don't lay out a strategy and plan to keep more money in their pocket. Good thing you found this book because I am going to challenge you to save money, if you really want to. (Though you've already read this far into the book so you must be serious about making a financial change.)

Remember, I am by no means a money expert and I have never claimed to be. I'm just a person who has learned the value of every penny and found ways to keep more of them in my bank account. Having said that, here is my strategy that I used and it saved me a lot of money in the first year.

Work backwards. How much do you want to save in a year? January is almost here but look ahead to next December and how much savings do you want to have? What are you going to do each month to achieve that goal?

Map out the year and figure out when your costs are higher than other months. December could be a lot because of holidays. Perhaps you have several family birthdays in the summer. Think about when you will need to spend more and when you can save more.

It is realistic to tell yourself you can save a few dollars every week. Challenge yourself to do more. We all have luxury and entertainment expenses that we are hesitant to do without. Maybe you can do without a couple of them certain times of the year.

Think about summertime and the time you'll spend at the lake, or worse yet at home flipping through the TV channels and complaining nothing is on. Strip down your cable service for the months you will be away. If you average a lot of lake time in July and August and your monthly cable bill is forty dollars, you just saved eighty dollars for the two months you will be out of town.

Same goes for your phone bill. If your home phone will be collecting dust for the time you are away, have it disconnected – or at least cut out the features that are irrelevant when you aren't there. Remember, some phone companies charge for all the extra features such as call waiting and voice mail. If you have a cellphone, that might be just as good for the summer.

Summer can be a time to recoup and get your finances in order for the last part of the year. You can look at your spending from January to June and see if your spending has gone up or down. Use the summer months to leverage and get yourself back on track for a season of savings.

In January people often spend less because of going all out for the holidays. This is a good time to practice your savings skills. Test that willpower when it comes to opening your wallet.

When you pay your bills each month, really look at the charges and see if the payments you make are necessary. Do you have services that cost you a monthly fee that you don't use? Why are you keeping them? Is it just easier to pay the few bucks a month as opposed to cancelling? That few minutes to cancel a service will save you money in the end.

Month by month you can come up with a plan of attack that might seem like a little extra cash here and there but you always have to look at the grand scheme of things and how much collectively you will save.

Don't tell yourself you will save tens of thousands of dollars in a year because if it doesn't happen you will feel like a failure. Go little by little. Set realistic targets. Tell yourself each paycheck you will put aside money towards paying off debt or into a savings account. Let's say five dollars for each. You've just spent ten dollars per paycheck for something that can save your credit. Good credit, as you might agree, is priceless.

Once you've worked your way through this book and the creative juices are flowing, I am certain you'll be able to find ways to save hundreds of dollars a year by making little lifestyle changes. Keep reading though, we're not done yet!

Let's tackle that getting-in-shape resolution. Don't think you can brush that one aside to focus on money saving. Because exercising at home and using things around the house is what will lead you to fulfilling your resolution of saving more money.

Gym memberships seem like a good idea: they put you in an environment with a bunch of health nuts and that is meant to motivate you to look like the ripped and toned people you see working out all around you. But let's get back to reality because a gym isn't always fun. If anything, it can be an intimidating place that can easily make you feel unwelcome if you don't look the part.

Scrap the expensive one-year or six-month membership and stay home. No, that doesn't mean stay home and sit on the couch, but if you are sitting on the couch while holding soup cans and doing arm curls I might cut you some slack.

There is no need to buy dumbbells and expensive workout equipment for your home because you undoubtedly have items that can help you get in shape. Whether that is cans of soup or a chair to lift or use to balance yourself to do leg squats, your home is already a gym even though you might not be aware of it.

TV is a good source of motivation. Tell yourself that you can watch TV all night if you are exercising the whole time. That might mean you are standing and doing squats or leg raises during commercial breaks or simply stretching or lifting until the next commercial break, there are things you can do without the gym membership.

Think of the workout equipment at the gym and what it has you doing. You might be laying or standing or sitting. This is where your creativity comes into play to figure out alternatives at home. Remember, if you are just starting out at the gym, you don't need the heavy lifting bar at this point.

There are dozens of workout DVDs at stores – and even free videos online – that give you a routine for getting in shape. Finding one that suits your skills and abilities can be beneficial, however, you can also come up with your own.

Figure out how long your workout will be. Remember there are two ways to look at it: how long you want to exercise and how long realistically you will exercise. Meet somewhere in the middle to challenge yourself.

Once you have determined the timing, come up with a "mix tape" of songs that will motivate you to do the work. Up-tempo beats are good for jogging in place or going out for a run. If you have given yourself the goal of a thirty-minute walk or run, come up with a play list that is that length and don't stop until you have gone through all the music.

Taking it one step further and incorporating a walk-run mix is ideal. Remember, you don't need a treadmill or nice weather to exercise at home.

Use one song to walk around or jog in place. The second song can be used for stair climbing. Third song is back to walking or jogging. Mixing it up and using music motivators will help you get through your workout.

When I am at home it is a rule that I don't sit while I talk on the phone. Depending on who is calling it could be a long chat and I make myself walk through the house throughout the entire conversation. It is only after I hang up the phone and look at the call counter that I am shocked to see I have been walking around for an hour. Who said gabbing on the phone all night is a waste of time?

MY FUNNY, THRIFTY VALENTINE

I realize my earlier rant about the word "thrifty" might seem contradictory to this chapter, but let's be honest, the most romantic day of the year can go without the word "cheap" – just this once though.

It's the thought that counts. Hopefully you have a partner that understands and appreciates that. If not, you might want to start saving up for Valentine's Day. Or, you wow your loved one with the time and effort it will take to pull off a romantic February fourteenth.

The trick to a memorable Valentine's Day is in the planning. Planning is key to saving money but also making it a special day for your partner. Oftentimes the onus is put on one partner to treat the other to a day of romance but you know what, it's a two-way street these days and the lovin' has got to go both ways.

One of you can take the lead and come up with a plan of what to do. Sometimes it feels like a low-key sort of year and other times it can be a full day or weekend of togetherness.

The focus should always be on the togetherness so as not to lose sight of the real purpose of Valentine's Day.

Ordering in food is one idea but why not have a fun night of naughty cooking? Get some candles and strip down to your cooking attire (you decide the dress code, not me. I'm not taking responsibility for you getting a grease burn on your delicates!) and have a romantic cooking lesson. It might even lead to a playful food fight. Either way, dining in is almost always cheaper than eating out.

If you live in a climate that has snow on Valentine's Day, head outside and make a snowman. Like a food fight, this might also lead to some contact as you wrestle each other in the snow. Remember to get your camera and take goofy pictures with your new snow friend. Maybe make two snowmen and have a couple frosty friends in the yard. If you don't have a yard, go to a local park and make some snow creatures.

After all, who said a snow formation has to be a snowman or woman? Make an animal of some sort. Challenge or dare your partner to come up with a snow dinosaur or snow dog.

Once you get a little too cold, there's nothing like coming inside for some warmth. If your partner loves bubble baths, go out and get a bottle of it if you don't already have some. It might set you back a few bucks but it will lead to a few hours of romance.

If you want to get a little goofy, spontaneously write a poem about your relationship where you and your partner each take turns saying a line. It would be fun to write it down but maybe just as romantic in the bathtub while blowing bubbles at each other.

The trick is to enjoy the moment and do what feels natural. Most people don't take the day off work to have Valentine's Day, so often the celebration is only meant to last a few hours anyway. Between your naughty cooking lesson and the snow party concluding with bathtub bubbles, you pretty much have your night set and it cost you next to nothing.

THE SECRETS TO INEXPENSIVE
BIRTHDAY FUN

It's another year older and another dollar spent. Birthdays can be fun but behind the scenes it can be a hassle to plan and pull off a great birthday. Naturally a child's birthday is more involved than an adult but it all depends on what you have planned.

We'll get to a child's birthday later in this chapter.

As people get older they generally want less attention on their birthday so it can be easy to get away with not having a big expensive party. Unless it is a milestone – forty, fifty, sixty-five – grownup birthdays are a thing of the past.

Surprise parties can be fun but many decisions need to be made before pulling off the shocker. How many people are you going to invite and can the guest list be trimmed to make the event cheaper? People often view a packed room as a positive because it shows a lot of people turned out to celebrate your special day, but if the attendees aren't on your list of faves, perhaps having a more intimate exclusive party is better.

The trick to a good surprise party is coordinating people the birthday guy or gal wouldn't suspect. Being able to introduce a surprise guest is more exciting than pulling a fast one with a party. It has happened to me that it is my birthday and all is quiet most of the day. It totally screams that a surprise is in the works. If anything you sit and wonder all day who is scheming and what they have planned so you might not enjoy the actual surprise when it happens.

Rather than spending time worrying about the soon-to-be-surprised victim, and getting them to the secret location without the cover being blown or making sure nobody blabs the secret, you might consider shifting what the actual surprise is. A surprise guest list aside from a surprise event can make the day more special.

I got the idea several years ago at Christmas when the surprise for my grandma was a long-lost grandson coming to see her and spending the day with the family. Sure, the celebration was going on but the big smile (and watery tears really kicked in) when the ultimate surprise was revealed and a distant relative showed up.

The old adage is true when it comes to birthdays: it is the thought that counts. I am not suggesting flying in someone from across the country as a birthday gift, but someone the birthday guy or gal wouldn't expect to show up at the party. And while this could be a set up for an awful prank, keep it something that will make for good crying photos where you can be a hero that you pulled off a nice and memorable surprise.

When it comes to gifts – just like my Christmas advice – think economically when presenting your present. Are you buying the person something they need or will even use? Are you getting something just for the sake of getting them something? Making it means more and that can be a cheaper but also more meaningful gift they will get.

Save money on cards. Seriously, I think many people these days are hitting up a dollar store to buy a cheap card than the ones with an overpriced flashy greeting card price tag. It didn't take me long to realize that I am not a card person. I don't like receiving cards and I don't like giving them. That stemmed from the feeling that cards are simply a waste. Sure, if someone is giving you cash or a lottery ticket, the card will come in handy, but so too will a plainly decorated envelope with your name written across it.

If the sentiment of a card is required, there are so many desktop publishing programs that assist in the creation and printing of a friendly greeting. This way you can customize the message and put a personalized touch on the design. Maybe there is an inside joke you have that would never be printed on a store-bought card. Making a card is cheaper and the laugh is louder when you skip the store and do it yourself.

I also gave up on wrapping paper years ago. In the years I have lived in my house I have never once wrapped a birthday gift. It is just as easy to reuse a gift bag and save money instead of glossy wrapping paper that will be torn to shreds and thrown out moments later. I have given a gift wrapped with the comic section of the newspaper. There is a lot of imagery and some color that makes it look like wrapping paper.

As for the kids: there is a lot of expectation when the youngsters have a birthday party. Whether it is the hope the celebration will take place at a fun play area or that there will be dozens of friends and lots of junk food, there are ways around the cost of throwing a great shindig.

A misconception would be that having a party at home is cheaper, but factoring in the food, decoration and other costs, you can be better off going to a location that is set up specifically for hosting such events.

The real cost saving happens if you visit an amusement establishment and an admission is charged. Oftentimes the kid play places host birthdays and they provide a lot of the entertainment. For the cost of a child coming to participate, you can generally get a package deal where snacks and games are included.

For instance if there is an indoor go-kart track with video games and mini golf, inquire about booking a birthday party with a special banquet room where you can set up home base and the kids are free to enjoy an afternoon of energy-burning entertainment. You might be responsible for bringing the cake but if the place has a snack bar, sometimes that is included in the price of renting a room.

At the risk of sounding like a broken record, do your research and planning. Find out which scenario works best for you. If you are having a simple gathering with a few family and friends, then a party at home might be a good idea. If there is a group of schoolmates coming for an afternoon of fun, the cost of going out and partially offsetting the cost onto the children's parents might be the way to go if the establishment helps with the party supplies and planning.

VACATIONING ON THE CHEAP

Everybody likes to take a vacation now and then, but it can prove to be costly. The common route is to go directly to the big airlines and book a vacation based on the flashy pictures and luxurious promises of the resort. A lot of people go the all-inclusive route, which I'll touch on in just a bit, but what about doing all the planning and coordinating yourself?

A growing number of discount travel websites is appearing. Gone are the days of paying full retail price for a vacation when for a fraction of the cost you can get the exact same vacation package on a lesser-known website.

Case in point: A recent return trip to New York City would have cost between one-thousand dollars and fourteen-hundred dollars on the major airline websites. Checking out discount travel websites like Expedia and Travelocity offered up essentially the same packages. Much to my surprise, there were several other similar websites that had deals cheaper than the cheaper sites.

But digging a little further and finding a site called CheapOAir, I was amazed that the trip people could be paying over a thousand dollars for I was able to book for about six-hundred dollars.

Granted, this didn't include hotel or car rental, but for less than half the price I was able to get to New York and use the money I saved for sightseeing adventures.

As I travel a fair bit, my brother called and told me he was booking a Disney vacation for his family. He said he only checked out the major airlines' websites and was ready to book at the suggested price. He was unaware discount travel sites existed.

I insisted he do his research and a few days of planning to determine exactly what he would have time for and what he wanted to do in Orlando. After some preliminary itinerary building, he came up with a schedule that found he wouldn't have had time to do everything originally put forth in the package deal he found on the airline's vacation website.

On a discount travel website he ended up saving approximately twenty-two-hundred dollars for his family of four to travel to Florida.

When it comes to more bang for your buck, a great choice is to visit an all-inclusive resort. A couple years ago I was able to book a week-long trip to Mexico. The cost of the trip included airfare, shuttle to the resort, the stay at the resort and all meals and alcohol. The base price before taxes and insurance was about four-hundred dollars. Yes, four-hundred for a week in Mexico where I didn't have to pay for food or booze the whole time.

Vacation websites have taxes and fees and will throw extra add-ons at you but going without them will keep the costs down. Many employers have travel insurance as part of an employee's benefits package which could cover you for international travel. That ended up saving me roughly one-hundred dollars at the time of booking.

All told the week in Mexico – that I didn't have to fuss or worry about the logistics of the trip – was well worth the just-over five-hundred-dollar price tag. Even without the hassle of planning from start to finish, you'd be hard-pressed to find a way to visit hotspots for that cheap with everything included. If you take into account the cost of only a hotel for a few nights (minus food, drinks, etc.) you are still better off to go all-inclusive for the duration of your stay.

The resort in Mexico felt like a community of friends. We all arrived at the airport together, we all bonded on the plane, we all checked in together, so it was comfortable and we all got to know each other the first day. We were staying amongst a cluster of resorts but at our location there were several ocean-side pools, a few restaurants, a spa, nightly entertainment, a discotheque and business center to check in with everybody at home and change your Facebook status to make everybody jealous.

There was a lot to do at the resort but the tour operator – that had an information table staffed around the clock to help us – provided a list of extra activities such as catamaran tours, watersports and trips into town. While fun, they are an added cost, so be warned you might want to consider getting local currency. I didn't convert any money because I assumed being all-inclusive I wouldn't have to buy anything so there was no need and I wasn't expecting to take part in the fun. I just wanted to lay on the beach and do nothing.

For those who still want the luxury of going to a tropical destination and staying in resort-like accommodations, a cruise is also one way to go.

While the ship is moving in the daytime you are enjoying the many amenities of the cruise line's facilities. Today's cruise ships have nightclubs, pools, waterslides – essentially complete amusement parks. So you really can do a bit of this and a bit of that. You will often stop in for the day at a beach-side dock and spend the day experiencing the location. You will board the ship in the evening and head off for another adventure.

A cruise ship is much more enjoyable than sitting on a plane for eight hours flying to your vacation spot (although oftentimes you end up having to fly to the departure city if you don't live nearby). On the ship you can party and enjoy the travels without so much as realizing you're even going anywhere. The problem with taking a cruise – if you don't live near the dock – is you still have to fly to the departure city which comes with an added cost (depending on your travel arrangements).

Cruises can be pricey but it depends on what you want to do and how you actually get there.

If you are fine with a standard room (and I always say the room is the least important part of the trip if you are on vacation) a cruise doesn't have to be expensive, seeing as meals and non-alcoholic beverages are included. All you'd need is spending money for gift shops, spas or local stores when docked.

Being a single, my biggest concern going on a Disney cruise was that there would be screaming kids everywhere. I must admit I was surprised and quite pleased when I learned the adults-only facilities included bars, pools and spas.

Much like airline tickets, spots on cruises get more expensive as the boat fills up and as departure date draws near. If you are an advanced planner you can book up to two years ahead of time, in some cases. This can also be risky because you never know if you will miss out on a promotion or sale price leading up to your cruise.

Airplane tickets are also a factor when considering a cruise. It's not as simple as booking a spot on the boat and you're sailing. If you live in the middle of the country you still need to somehow get to the coast. Flights during peak times are very expensive. It is important to consider booking flights to the cruise ship departure location as an added expense that could possibly double the cost of your trip.

Hopefully this isn't information overload and hasn't taken the fun out of your vacation planning. But to maximize your dollar and your fun, you must consider exactly what you want to do on the trip. If you are going to enjoy the sun and escape to do nothing, a vacation can be very cheap. Also, it would be unnecessary to stay at a place that is known to be a flashy tourist hotspot.

If you are vacationing for sightseeing and adventure, plan your trip with that in mind. Of course, you can do what I did in Mexico and just wing it the whole time which makes for an entirely different adventure altogether. Going with the flow is exciting but as I learned, it ends up being a lot more expensive, however if you have a long flight before you get to the final destination, you can always do some thinking and planning of how you will spend your days which will make you look even more forward to your trip.

You can't go wrong with enlisting the help of a travel agent. They know ways to go about planning a trip for exactly what you want to do. A vacation shouldn't be stressful to plan or to take so if you'd rather not have to worry about any of the details, trust in a travel professional to get you there.

Think before you spend. Vacations are doable but you don't need to go broke to have a fabulous time during your travels.

THE HOTEL GAME

So you are planning the family vacation and the first thing you need to do is book a hotel. The natural instinct would be to go to your favorite hotel's website and make a reservation. Stop! There's a few things you need to know first.

Hotels often list something as a "best rate guarantee." Those three words are very important and they work in your favor.

It's not difficult to find discount travel websites – as I mentioned previously – so this is where your online researching skills come into play. You'll need to have a few open browser windows for this. And comparative shopping actually becomes fun, if not a challenge.

Let's say you go to Hotel A's website. They have a rate of two-hundred dollars per night for rooms. You go to Travel Website A's page and they have it for one-hundred-ninety dollars per night. Then you go to Travel Website B's page and they have it for one-hundred-sixty-five dollars per night. This is where the fun begins.

Each of the three websites offers to match or beat the lowest advertised price. It might take some back and forth but if you are lucky you can get a huge discount on every night you stay at the hotel.

I tried this with one hotel whose website had a "best rate guarantee" but when I called to get additional details, the front desk agent knew nothing about it – even going as far as telling me they didn't have a policy. Further still, after looking at his own hotel's website he still said it didn't exist.

A manager told me nobody had ever taken up the hotel on its policy so the employee was uninformed. The hotel was prepared to match the lowest price and offer a ten percent discount on the competitor's lowered price to officially beat the lowest advertised price. Had I just booked on the hotel's website, I would have paid the regular rate. One Toronto hotel even offered a free night and to match a competitor's rate if it was advertised lower elsewhere.

The trick is to search around for hotels in the area where you are staying or even off the beaten path that are still close by where you plan to spend your vacation time.

Take for instance a place like New York's Times Square. Hotel rates there are ridiculous. But there are plenty of hotels off Broadway and still within walking distance (or at least a quick, cheap cab ride away) and you can enjoy the benefits of sightseeing without the annoyance of Times Square's constant noise and sirens.

In the past I called a hotel making it seem like I was looking for accommodations for a large group. "Do you have many rooms available for such-and-such night?" I asked roughly how many rooms were available (again, not lying to them, but having them think I had a large reservation for them) and I flipped it around and asked for a deal seeing as they had so much vacancy.

"Why not sell out the room for cheap if it's just going to be sitting empty anyway? A paying guest is a paying guest, right?" And voila, I got a really cheap place to stay.

Booking hotels has become a game since there is never a definite fixed rate for rooms. Play it to your advantage and you will be surprised at the luxurious accommodations for next to nothing.

PETS TAKE THEIR OWN VACATION

The excitement is building for the upcoming vacation but there's a few little details to take care of: who is going to look after the pets?

It is like leaving your kids. Do you stick them with just anybody?

Pet-sitting can be stressful. If you have a hyperactive puppy you might find friends who don't mind watching the pooch for a few hours here and there but the same people are full of excuses why they can't help you out for a full day or two, much less a week.

While we might get mad, think about how you'd feel in the same situation. You aren't a pet fan and then you have this dog in your face annoying you and never leaving you alone. Can we blame people for rejecting the request?

None of your family and friends is willing to stay at your place to constantly monitor the animals so a kennel is the next idea. Bring out the Yellow Pages and start looking up local boarders. The fear really begins now.

How do you know it is a reputable place that is going to take care of your furry family member? Will there be exercise and interaction or will they just be locked in a cell like some common prisoner?

Checking out kennel websites and seeing the accommodations can help ease the nerves – a little bit. Some places have webcams in the kennels and you can log in online and watch streaming video of your pet. (Probably not a good idea since you'll find it hard to pull yourself away from the computer while you are gone – but it's a feature that might help you sleep better at night.)

Kennels can be expensive. If you are paying somebody twenty dollars, forty dollars or even fifty dollars per day, you expect them to be spending lots of time with your dog, giving them attention and affection and not just walking up and down a hallway like a warden to check in on them from time to time.

There are dog-sitting services where someone will stay at your home – and also take care of plants, coincidentally. It's said this option is less stressful for a pet seeing as they are still in their own environment. Again, it's a matter of deciding whether or not that is worth the money and the comfort knowing the pet will have a new friend to show around your place.

There are doggy daycares that have a group of animals socializing throughout the day while owners are at work. Many of them offer boarding which means the pets can stay overnight and have new friends to play with each day.

I send my dog to a farm where the owner has an animal rescue and doggy daycare. During my last trip she had fifteen dogs staying on a long weekend and my dog didn't even want to come home with me when I picked him up. OK, that part was a little heartbreaking, but he was so tired from running around all day that I felt good he had a fun time. There are no cages, no restrictions. The dogs are in the house, on the furniture and it's just like home but in a different place.

Several options are available for pet care while you are away and it is one of those instances where you need to consider what makes you comfortable and what you feel is a reasonable price to pay for your pet.

WHEN YOU'RE LEAVING ON A JET PLANE

Your bags are packed and you're ready to go. But how much are the bags packed and how much will that cost you?

If you're like me, the first few trips I went on I loaded up my suitcase and crammed it with clothes for every occasion in every type of weather.

I had runners for long walks, dressy shoes for a night out, sandals for the beach. That's just the footwear.

Next is the jeans for an afternoon of sightseeing, the shorts for a hot day, the swimsuit for the beach, the dressy pants for dinner and a show; the T-shirts, the sweatshirts, the jackets. You see where I'm going with this, right?

Before you know it the suitcase is full and you have trouble zipping it up, and once it is you hope the zip doesn't break.

Take into consideration what you will be doing on your trip. Are you doing any shopping? How are you getting home with all your newly purchased goodies? If the suitcase was jam-packed before you even left home, how are you going to manage bringing it all back with you?

Buying another suitcase and filling that with your purchases is one idea, but with most airlines charging passengers to check their luggage, it can be expensive.

One idea is to mail yourself the items. Postage can be less expensive but it still does the trick. It might take a bit longer to get to you, however saving money without having to pay for extra luggage on the plane might be more appealing.

Most airlines allow for up to two carry-on bags. They suggest keeping personal electronics and other valuables with you to ensure there is no damage to or loss of your personal belongings. The pockets and compartments can store extra pairs of socks and underwear to save space in the actual luggage you are paying to check underneath the plane.

Gone are the days of wheeling into the airport and taking with you clothes you'll never wear and things you'll never use. Being compact equals being inexpensive with today's airline travel.

YOU'RE ON VACATION, NOW WHAT?

Once you are on vacation, what can you do to save money? You're already there – now what?

Let's take New York City, for instance. Times Square welcomes thousands of tourists every day. The natural thought would be to book a hotel, eat and spend your money in Times Square. Wrong, wrong, wrong!

Like any good tourist trap, prices are incredibly inflated in Times Square. Some restaurants charge a fortune for what you would pay almost half the price for elsewhere.

One restaurant featured a twenty-dollar salad when it is nowhere close to that price at other restaurants in the chain. In fact, it's only about twelve dollars at its other locations.

Souvenir stands are everywhere. Be careful about buying at the first folding table you come across. "Hand-painted" scenic pictures of New York seem authentic at the first stand but as you stroll down Broadway or approach Central Park, you quickly see the same picture over and over. And as you might expect, each has different prices.

Starting out the pictures are fifteen dollars, then two for twenty-five dollars, then ten dollars each. Shop around. And don't be afraid to dicker with the price. I only had a twenty-dollar bill and wanted two pictures and it didn't take much arm-twisting to get the seller to agree to my negotiated price.

Furthermore, there are dozens – if not hundreds – of souvenir shops. Not that I'm saying to avoid the ones in Times Square, but a short walk down Broadway and you can find the typical "I heart NY" shirts priced at four for ten dollars. In some stores they are anywhere from fifteen dollars to forty dollars.

It's a little bit of a stroll but if you're already out sightseeing anyway, there's no harm in that few extra steps. And if you have to walk back from where you came, you can always stop back at the first stores if nothing else tickled your fancy.

Elsewhere, on street corners there are ticket sellers for everything – Broadway shows, bus tours and comedy shows. Most of the sellers are legitimate but a good idea is to check out offers on the Internet. Sometimes you can score cheap tickets and good deals on different packages. There are no less than forty ticket websites I found just with an online search.

TRAVEL'S TRAVELS

So you're on vacation and you need to get around. How are you going to do it?

Renting a car seems cheap, so why not? But a quick assessment of your travel needs when, well, travelling can end up saving you a lot of money.

You get to the airport, the car rental place is there, and it's easiest to just pick up a vehicle and be on your way.

Are you going to a place where public transportation is reliable and efficient? Somewhere such as Los Angeles most people drive. Everything is so stretched out in Los Angeles County that you could be riding a bus for hours to get from point A to point B. Most L.A. residents would tell you to rent a car.

But someplace such as Orlando where there is essentially a tourist district and one trolleybus can pick you up at your hotel and take you to the amusement park for a dollar-fifty.

And most of the theme parks aren't too far from each other, so a bus ride or cab ride isn't too expensive.

New York City has lots of places to see but it's a cluster of tourist attractions in Times Square. All you need is a cheap airport shuttle (roughly twenty-two dollars for a round trip from the airport to the hotel and back) and that's all the added transportation costs you have. This route might take a little longer than renting a car, but sharing a van with a few other people and not having to worry about navigating congested streets and just relaxing while you are driven by somebody might be more appealing, not to mention cheaper.

The trick to cheap vacations is all in the planning. Map out everything that will happen and how it is going to happen. Every little detail from "are we going to drive or just cab it?" to "do we get expensive room service at the hotel or clip coupons before we get there and save at area restaurants?" must be factored in to ensure a reasonably priced vacation.

Trip planning starts before you even leave home. It might take a lot of extra legwork at the beginning but if it is all properly coordinated you'll have a great time because you did your homework and saved.

Happy travels!

MAKING SOME MONEY

THE ART OF ONLINE GARAGE SALES

While I am hesitant to call my friend a hoarder (because there's a good chance he's reading this book), he certainly is a packrat. Old computers stacked in a corner of the living room. Empty jewelry boxes he "knows for sure" will one day come in handy. But my friend turned over a new leaf. He decided to rid himself of his one-time treasures and make some cash.

Gone are the days of garage sales and sitting outside for a few hours hoping people will come by and pick through your belongings. Thanks to the Internet, you can sell things to people outside your neighborhood.

My friend lives in a cramped Chicago apartment. It is a two-bedroom place with three people living in it. If you thought you were tight for space, you haven't seen these living arrangements.

As the actual renter my friend was looking for roommates. He had to downsize considerably to make room for his fellow dwellers. That meant he needed to hit eBay and craigslist to liquidate his unneeded assets.

It was a walk down memory lane as my friend picked through boxes he had in storage and hadn't seen in nearly ten years. He had everything from a dart board (though admitted he couldn't remember ever playing darts) a pair of skates (he's had bad knees for years so doesn't know when he last skated) and several items that he could say adios to.

He listed about forty items online and within minutes was getting responses from interested buyers. My friend was shocked to realize there would be so many people in Chicago that would be tuned into item-selling websites.

Responding to inquiries, he had interested people swing by the apartment to check out the items from his online garage sale, and ended up clearing out a quarter of the things he listed. (I am leery about letting strangers into my place, but that's an individual choice.)

All told he made about eight-hundred-fifty dollars from his spring cleaning/fundraising sale. So what's he going to do with that money? He said he will put up shelving and display some of the trophies he won in school that he forgot he had.

The stuff you can find in storage, hey?

GET PAID FOR YOUR HOBBY

Everybody has a talent. And if reality TV has taught us anything, it's that there are plenty of ways to cash in on what we do.

I fall short of using the word "exploit" but if you know what you're good at, find a way to make money at it.

With the economy leaving many people strapped for cash, the decision might be to reluctantly look for a second job. You'll find yourself skimming the help wanted section and saying, I guess I could do that. No enthusiasm, just a groan that you believe you can tolerate the position for a short time to make some extra cash.

Assess your skills and see if you can be your own part-time boss. There are plenty of stay-at-home moms with their own businesses to make some extra cash.

A woman in Grand Forks, N.D. who makes homemade soaps and bath products; a woman in Missoula, Mon. who creates decorated sugar cookies; a woman in Hamilton, Ont. who teaches folk dancing. All three are making decent money without it seeming like work. These women have one thing in common – no, not just that they adore their kids (of course) – but that their hobby is now making them money.

All it takes is posting an ad for your services on a community billboard at the local grocery store and your phone could soon be ringing with people wanting to take you up on your offer. And if it's anything like the women I referenced, you'll need staff, a bigger kitchen and a big smile on your face when the cash starts coming in.

If you are good at something, teach others to do it. If you are an expert with a skill you can teach people what you know – and make money.

There is nothing wrong with charging people to learn from you. Many community centers offer programming to the neighborhood during the daytime and on evenings and weekends. You might have to rent the spot for a few bucks but if you get a group of people together and charge them seven or eight bucks for a one-hour yoga session, you've just made some good coin for sixty minutes of work. And if there is a lot of interest, host two sessions per week and you might even be able to earn a week's salary in two hours just for teaching people your hobby.

While many people write poetry or short stories as a hobby, the world of self-publishing is becoming increasingly popular. Websites like iTunes and Amazon make it easy for you to promote and sell your creations to the world. Back in the day it would cost an arm and a leg to publish your own novel but now companies make it easier for you to do it – sometimes with no cost at all – and they just take a cut of your sales.

Factoring in what it would cost you to pay a company to print your book – and that might not even include design work or editing – you can put together your own material by designing your own cover, having friends and family proofread the work and only paying for copies you order and getting a royalty anytime your project is sold online.

All those poems you wrote about past relationships and short stories you wrote about your life could make you a few bucks here and there and it's a bonus to have that extra cash come in.

Many people expect to make a living from writing and selling one book but that is highly unlikely without the backing of a major publishing house. The publishing industry is set up so it is difficult for a writer to get a book deal without the help of a literary agent. And getting that type of representation also doesn't cost you anything.

Pitching yourself to an agent is usually free (it's said if you have to pay upfront that the dealings could be shifty and should be avoided). There will be lots of rejection because agents are bombarded with queries every day, but depending on how serious you are about being a published writer it could be worth the effort. Remember, this chapter is covering how to make money from a hobby, not get rich from a hobby.

When I wrote my first book, I used my resourcefulness to coordinate local book signings and get the title on store shelves. Many bookstores welcome local writers and even have a special section devoted to homegrown talent. Some of the books are written by people hoping to make a career in writing, but there are lots of people buying local books just because they are local and those are often the most heartfelt stories when people write for the passion of doing it and not the dollars attached to it.

While it is difficult to land a top spot in major bookstores the local aspect is something to focus on. There are smaller bookstores that have a platform to support local writers so getting in good with those outlets is a great recommendation. Whether the store buys your book directly from you or carries it on a consignment basis, they are likely to help you out because they want to support you and also make money from the books. When it comes to national chains, there is so much room devoted to the big publishers it can be hard to get noticed.

I have heard from a few people that are involved in their community and been able to get their book sold at local grocery or corner stores. Again, the "little guy" has more appreciation for the other "little guy" and therefore the two support each other. You can never underestimate the importance of networking and building solid relationships with people and organizations.

Like the women I referenced earlier, you can use the Internet to your advantage and create a website to sell your book. There are many free templates and companies that provide transaction services where people can buy your book and you can automatically send them a digital file. That is sheer profit from each sale because there is no printing cost or shipping charges.

Later in the book I will outline how to get free publicity and national attention with no advertising costs whatsoever.

EFFECTIVE COMMUNICATING, COMPLAINING AND NEGOTIATING

GOING FOR THE KILL

Don't misunderstand this chapter. It's not about complaining for the sake of complaining. Letting a company know about your situation could really benefit you.

I first learned this as a child when I lost a dollar in a drink machine outside a local supermarket. It wasn't a huge loss but I felt ripped off when the store wouldn't do anything for me and staff referred me to the soft drink maker. I called up to report lost money in the machine and they sent me a coupon for a free six-pack of drinks.

Any way you want to look at it, I came out ahead on that.

Again, I am in no way encouraging people to lie to companies about personal experiences, but letting them know could help in a resolution that ultimately makes you a happy customer.

The trick is to remember that at store level, sometimes there are limits to what can be accomplished. But taking it to the corporate level, well, that's a whole new game.

Have you ever been upset about your cellphone bill with charges you don't understand – or worse yet, erroneous charges you shouldn't have had? Did you have to deal with a snotty customer service representative that told you his or her hands were tied and that you just better get over it? OK, maybe they didn't use that wording, but that was the gist of it.

It's funny how when you flex your muscle you can get what you want. If you know your facts and what you want to achieve by calling in, sticking to your guns can (usually, will) pay off in the end.

Think about it: you're on the receiving end of a call – you're that telephone operator. The customer calls and is hesitant and apologetic, almost nervous while explaining the situation. You can easily steamroll the customer and stay in control of the conversation. Now, imagine someone has their facts lined up, who can back up their statements and has the confidence that they mean business and is determined to get the problem resolved to their satisfaction. That one you might not want to challenge.

So let's say you go over on your daytime minutes or your data and you call to complain about overage charges because you didn't know the limits (and again, you legitimately didn't know, as I am not suggesting lying to companies). Maybe you go for sympathy and the "poor me, I didn't know" route. Or maybe you stand your ground and say it wasn't made clear to you that your limit was being reached and you should be notified. Either way, you have a goal in mind: have the charges reversed.

More often than not a customer service agent will tell you there is nothing that can be done. Sometimes asking for a supervisor can get you partway to your goal. But what if that doesn't work? There's got to be someone else to turn to.

In the case of many cellphone companies, you can always ask to speak to customer relations. If all else fails, implying that you will cancel your service gets you put through to an entirely different department that can do anything to your account.

With so much competition these days in the cellphone world, it's unlikely a company will call your bluff and say, "OK, we'll cancel your service" without making a last-ditch effort to keep you as a customer.

Last year I challenged the monthly "system access fee" charged by my cellphone service provider. My argument: I have been a customer for over ten years and have paid it every month, but somebody new getting a phone – not even locked in with a contract – doesn't have to pay it.

It was a logical argument. Obviously the phone rep had been groomed on this type of call, considering a class-action lawsuit was threatened years ago. The rep told me that new price plans have the access fee worked into the total cost and the people are technically paying it. Either way, that's a misleading statement that I also raised as an issue.

Getting nowhere with the customer service agent I asked to speak to a supervisor. After a long wait I spoke with someone who had a solution for me: they waive the monthly access fee. That wasn't so hard, was it?

But a year later I noticed the charge back on my account. I called in after noticing the charge on the bill and I was told the credit was for one year. That was never told to me and if I wanted it again I would have to renew my contract for another three years. I explained that I was never told the length of the credit – going so far as telling them to look back in the account and even listen to the original call (because when I am that certain, they must know I mean business, right?) but they told me they didn't have a record of the call from that far back. Seeing as they can't back up their own claim, I would benefit.

Still refusing to accept a six-dollar monthly charge, I fought contract renewal stipulation and also wanted credit for the months I had unknowingly paid the fee. When that became a fight I casually asked when my contract was up for renewal. Coincidentally it was a few months away. I asked to speak to customer relations about the problem since it would be nothing for me to cancel my service and go with someone else – reminding them at the same time I'd been a customer for over ten years and have a long history of expensive phone bills – meaning they would be losing a lot of money without me as a customer.

Isn't it remarkable how stating your case, standing your ground and not being pushed around can work in your favor? If I had gone into the call with lack of information and no documentation (example: the date of the first call regarding the problem, a reference number and the name of the customer service agent) I could have easily been steamrolled and brushed off so the operator could get to the next call. Instead, I made a big deal because I knew I was right. I knew I hadn't been told about the timeframe so I challenged the company and it couldn't back up its own statements and prove to me I was wrong.

There are a lot of people that won't bother to make an issue of a minor charge on their account but one way to look at it is thinking about the millions of other customers with a minor charge and how much the company could be profiting because of people sitting quietly and not doing anything about it.

If that's not motivation enough to defend the money you worked for, I don't know what is. In the long run, six dollars per month over the course of ten years is over seven-hundred dollars. It's worth looking closer at all your bills and making sure they are on the up and up. Too many companies want customers to change to automatic payments, suggesting it is easier than manually paying each bill. But in doing so, consumers had best be reviewing monthly bills when they arrive to make sure there are no erroneous charges.

I happened to notice the six-dollar charge returned to my cellphone bill four months after it came back. The only reason I looked at the bill closely that month was because I wanted to see a long-distance plan I bought a month earlier for international travel had been applied correctly. (I previously bought one for twenty dollars, only to receive a text the day before I went away confirming my thirty-dollar purchase. You guessed it, another call to the company. This time they listened back to the call from days earlier and confirmed I was given incorrect information and they had to honor what I was told.)

THE SOFTER APPROACH

The same thing can be said for being unsatisfied with a purchase. Maybe not completely unsatisfied, but you aren't fully happy.

You bought a new appliance and there's something minor that bothers you about it. You can make it known that you aren't happy with the exact one you have but would be willing to stay with the same brand, just a different model in the future. This is something that could be mentioned at store level, but maybe someone at the corporate office can help you out.

This is where a bit of brand butt kissing can help. Let's say it's a new microwave and you aren't fully impressed with its functionality. You could always call up the corporate office and say how much you really like the microwave but it's lacking this and that. You might ask for a suggestion about another one of the company's products that would best suit you. Going in attacking is not the best method for this type of request. You would just shoot yourself in the foot.

The pleasant approach is what is used because you aren't exactly angry about anything. If anything, you are wanting a step up from where you are. This is where you pull out the compliments and flattery to the public relations person you get on the phone.

This is not to say you'll be upgraded to the company's top-of-the-line model but you might at least be able to get a coupon or voucher for a future purchase. Remember, they want you to be a long-time customer. And since you've already spoken highly about your current purchase, they haven't had to do half the work like when a disgruntled customer calls in. You're already happy so they just need to do something minor to keep you there.

It's been proven that the friendlier you are to a customer service rep, the likelier they are to go the extra mile to help you. If you come out swinging, they might shut down and say there's nothing they can do. Your approach depends on the situation. In the cellphone instance, if you've dealt with the company before – or if it has a history of not bending to convenience customers – you have to be prepared for anything. But in the case of a microwave, you are simply testing the waters to see what you could get out of a company.

Being complimentary and endlessly grateful by constantly thanking them and pouring on the charm will probably get you far. I know from my years working in retail that if someone was argumentative that I would help them to the limits I was required to. But if they showed gratitude and were genuinely happy with what I'd done, I would often throw in extras that I didn't have to – sometimes extras that could have got me in trouble.

Either way, sticking up for what is right can greatly benefit you when dealing with big companies. The bottom line is it's your money, don't be so quick to toss your hands and say, "Ah, what are you gonna do?" Now you know what to do!

WANT A DISCOUNT? ASK FOR IT!

Some people are afraid to look cheap. All I have to say to that is: be cheap and be proud!

The thing to remember is that in many cases companies are profiting a lot more than what it costs to sell you the product. If you buy something for ten dollars, more often than not, the company paid less than half that amount for the product. Depending on where the product comes from, sometimes that retailer negotiated a discount by buying in large quantities.

If it's good enough for the company to ask for a deal, what's wrong with the consumer doing it?

Some people feel they are being pushy by asking for more and more, but the thing to remember is that once the deal is done and you've paid for a product or service, it couldn't hurt to ask for extras. Ask for free shipping, or ask for a coupon or discount on your next purchase. If anything, this tells the company that you'll be back and spending your money with them again.

Perhaps there is only one item left or the packaging is a little damaged yet you know there isn't anything wrong with the actual product. Why not ask for a percentage off because of the cosmetic packaging problem?

It is all about the timing. Going in for a discount without striking up conversation or forming a relationship with an employee probably won't work. It might if the employee is desperate for a sale, but oftentimes you'll get a big fat no if you expect to get everything under the sun just because you walked into the store and you are you. You are nobody to them, especially if the company won't profit from you.

If you are a repeat customer and can reference other things you bought from the company or ask questions about the current offering or, hell, even comment on their recent store renovation, it shows loyalty towards the company. It shows you are a regular and that could also increase your chance of a great discount.

You can also ask for an employee by name. Not that you are name dropping, but if the salesperson offered a great experience last time, you could help them get a good commission on the next sale. Also, if that particular employee is not there, you can deal with someone else and it still shows you are a dedicated customer.

It never hurts to ask questions about a product or service. If you are buying a product that requires a service, you have a perfect opportunity to jump the gun before the employee attempts the upsell and show you mean business by asking about any promotions or specials they might have about your product's servicing. Ask if there's a rebate or coupon they could give you.

Maybe it's happened to you at a grocery store that the friendly clerk knows something you are buying is on sale in a flyer and happens to have it right there and enters the code to give you the discount. You didn't know it was there but they sure did.

When I worked retail we would get the upcoming store flyer a week in advance. Sometimes we had it on the other side of the counter while talking to a customer. If I had built a relationship with the person, I would let them know that if they bought the item(s) the next day, they would save because it/they are going on sale.

Ask about related products or services surrounding your purchase and if there is anything that can be done about getting the price knocked down. It's worked before that simply by asking I got a free cleaning of my stove because the company had vouchers for first-time customers. Would I have been given one anyway? Not necessarily. But inquiring helped seal the deal.

Discounts aren't necessarily only for big purchases, as I described about a grocery store coupon. It's used in everyday life when ordering food, buying a car, booking a vacation. Even buying a house has some wheeling and dealing to it.

Let's take ordering pizza: you go to a restaurant's website and see the menu and its prices. You call to place an order but by simply asking about any other promotions not on the website, sometimes they can actually come up with a special for you. If you are only ordering food for one person, tell them you don't need a combo with two pizzas and wings and drinks. Tell them it's one person and what you need. Oftentimes they can hook you up with exactly what you want by mixing and matching without having to pay the regular price.

DISCOUNTS ARE GREAT, BUT FREE IS BETTER

It's amazing how you can get free things just by asking. A discount is great, but come on, who doesn't love free stuff?

The cable company always wants you to go for the biggest package: five-hundred channels, HD, and all the bells and whistles. But if you don't need it – like I don't – you can pick and choose just the channels you want.

Simply by asking, I got a free DVR because I was unsure about HD programming and considered going to another company for my TV service. I wasn't making up stories, I really was debating about staying with the current company that forced me to keep a bunch of channels I didn't want just for the sake of having two that I wanted.

All I did was ask what current promotions they had and I said I saw a commercial for their new high-end DVR. I said I would stay with them if they gave me one and I would consider the HD programming after a free-month trial. They part with a device that maybe cost them a hundred bucks or so and in that they retain me as a customer with the potential to upgrade to a more expensive service.

It doesn't always have to be big-ticket items. The best place to form positive business relationships is within your own community.

How many times have you been in need of something and you run to the corner store because it's the quickest and easiest place? Have you ever run out of something and just decided to spend a bit more for the convenience of picking it up down the street?

I usually get dog food from the big-box store quite a ways from my house. There have been times when I have run out of food and didn't want to go all the way there and battle the lines of customers just for one item. Instead I walked the dog to the corner pet store and ended up walking out of there with his belly full of treats and a free bag of dog food under my arm.

So how did that happen? First, I did not go in wearing a ski mask and demanding all the treats from the counter. I have taken the dog in there several times and the employees "know" us now.

We make small talk about the dog, he loves going to see the girls that work there. And through conversation about dog food, one of the employees mentioned the store has expired dog food in the back. They either take it home for their own pets or donate it to an animal shelter.

Don't get me wrong, I am all about giving to charity, but if the store's policy is they think of their own staff first, I shouldn't feel guilty about a free bag of dog food.

When the employee first told me about expired dog food I was concerned about its safety. When I looked at the date and saw it only expired a few days earlier, I was all for giving it to my dog since he'd devour it before it even got to the dogs at a shelter.

There I was standing in the pet store expecting to buy another expensive bag of dog food, but just by making chit chat and being a good customer in the past, I was rewarded with free chow for my pooch.

THE ART OF SHAMELESS SELF-PROMOTION

Almost anybody on Facebook knows it is a platform to brag about your life. As much as people don't want to admit it, it's all about look-at-me and look-what-I-do and look-how-cute-my-kids-are. You've seen it!

And while some people roll their eyes about the whole self-gratification of putting yourself on a pedestal and showcasing how wonderful you are, if you have a legitimate product or service to sell, there's nothing wrong with, well, excuse the term, whoring yourself.

For instance: you make crafts at home. You started it as a hobby (as described in an earlier chapter of this book) and you earn a few extra bucks here and there selling at area craft shows or to friends and family. But if you want to take it to the next level and be noticed, there is nothing wrong with seeking out free advertising avenues that are just as good as any paid advertising.

Everybody thinks of the traditional newspaper ad but how many people think to call up the newspaper and ask for a story written about them? It's true. If you have a small business operating out of your home, a community newspaper will probably want to tell others what you have accomplished. Instead of spending money to advertise in that paper, the paper is paying somebody to interview you and promote your business. It doesn't get any better than that!

People know that anybody can take out an ad in the paper. All we think of when we see an ad is that the company had money to advertise. But when there is a positive fluffy story about your crafting business that started out as a hobby, the image is already set for you that you are a good person. It is unlikely a community paper would go in for the kill and dig up dirt on you, so you can count on a story as helping boost your advertising and maybe giving you a bit of confidence since the spotlight is shining on you for a brief time.

If the community paper is part of a bigger chain of daily metro newspapers, you might also get contacted by someone at the bigger paper, or even from a wire service where the story ended up. So here you are this crafty person at home now with national exposure just because of a story the local paper ran. Never underestimate the power of the Internet these days. Because if your original story was posted on the newspaper's website, you might be surprised how many Internet search results there are for you in a couple weeks.

If you feel like increasing your exposure, expand your reach and contact different crafting magazines with your story. If there was a positive response in the community paper, share that information with a larger industry-specific audience. Pitch a different story angle about amateur crafters making a hobby their career (or whatever might apply to your situation). The more ideas you can give them, the easier it will be for the publication to sign on to featuring you in an article.

So you've got print down, what about broadcast outlets? Depending on where you live, there could be a local radio show or public access TV show/channel that features people like you. All you need to do is find out who the contact is at the radio or TV station, either make a call or send a sample of your offerings and, again, ask for some airtime. You have to remember that community outlets – newspapers, TV, radio – are there for the community. They are intended to be a platform for people in the community. That's you!

Once you have some articles in well-known publications and/or appearances under your belt, this is when you can start to ramp up your promotional efforts. It is a good time to start giving samples or finding ways to get your offerings in the public eye.

Maybe there is a local craft show coming up, or you know somebody getting married and offer to make them items as giveaways. It doesn't hurt to take a risk on giving free products and conveniently including your business card for future purchases.

It's happened before where I was given cookies at a wedding and attached to the cellophane wrap was the maker's company name and contact info. At first I thought it was tacky but the cookies were great and it made me call up the company to make an order for an event I was hosting. Just getting that one order from a wedding could have proved a lucrative strategy for the cookie maker.

Silent auctions are becoming more and more popular. People are always asking for prize donations. If what you make is something that can be included in a prize basket, by all means, participate. This will get your product into the hands of the winner, it will get name recognition when the prize basket is announced and even if people didn't win, they might still remember your name and decide to look you up later and become a customer.

Remember, it might cost you a little upfront but the word-of-mouth from people impressed with your products could catapult you into mega sales. Look at how many people have been discovered by a celebrity and a ringing endorsement from the rich and famous can change their business, not to mention their life.

When Oprah's daytime talk show was on the air, people were clamoring to be featured because just a few words out of Oprah's mouth could crash your website and have your phones ringing off the hook.

Which brings me to the next point: contact celebrities in your industry.

True, you might not get Oprah's attention right away, but it is increasingly easy to catch a celeb's eye. With Facebook and Twitter and contact information on websites, many celebrities want to be more accessible and they are more interactive with people writing to them. Again, what's it going to hurt by tweeting a message or posting a Facebook message directed at your target in the hopes of them noticing?

Take it one step further: get names of people associated with the celebrity. Whether that's a producer, a creative designer – anybody that has access to the star – and attempt to make contact either on the star's website or looking up their profile on Facebook. (Hey, if you don't want people to search you out, don't be on Facebook with all your personal information.

If you don't want us to know you're an executive producer on that particular show, don't put it as public info!)

Some people might see this as a daunting task, but if you look at it as a mission or goal for the success of your product offering, you'd be surprised how motivating it can be. As an entrepreneur you are told not to take no for an answer, and it's all about using your creativity to leverage your time in the spotlight.

GET GOING, GIRL!

This book is about ways to save you money and how to make a few bucks. If you weren't thinking so creatively before, I hope you see there are ways you can impact your wallet. It isn't necessarily about going without, rather simply cutting corners or using ingenuity to get through life.

The information I have given you is in no way meant to be a get-rich-quick scheme nor is it intended to be tips on how to scam companies or be deceitful to profit.

Some people might not have the patience to count every penny of savings, however if you make the effort to be more conscious of how you spend, you might not be quick to complain about being broke or short on cash.

Earlier I mentioned I have never been strapped for cash and I certainly can't say that it is because I am rich or even make a lot of money. It is the choices I have made along the way – and don't get me wrong, I have made several money mistakes – and used that newfound knowledge to have a positive impact on my finances.

While some of the ideas might seem far-fetched or unrealistic for your lifestyle, I encourage you to give them a chance. Originally I was embarrassed about some of my savings strategies but once I embraced my creativity I was fully comfortable telling people how I can have so much without having to be rich.

Money is often a touchy subject with people. It's a topic shooed under the rug. Remember, a lot of these tips are things nobody would even know you are doing so there shouldn't be any shame. At the same time, you might be surprised how impressed people are thinking you might be the next Martha Stewart or Suze Orman.

ABOUT THE AUTHORS

Jeremy Bradley is a Canadian syndicated newspaper columnist and radio host. His top 40 music show Top of The Charts earned Jeremy the distinction of outstanding talk media webcaster in 2010 and 2011 from Talkers magazine. In addition to his hosting duties, Jeremy is also an entertainment reporter for local morning radio shows.

Bonnie Winters is a former managing editor in the trade publishing industry. Bonnie is currently a producer at SpeakFree Media Inc., contributing to the success of the company's internationally syndicated radio shows and developing the company's book publishing projects.

www.speakfreemedia.com
www.speakfreebooks.com